EDUCATION: YOUR DESTINY'S VESSEL

ROSA GONZÁLEZ

The Biblical verses were taken from the New King James Version of the Bible. The names of the people in this book have been changed to protect the privacy. Any resemblance to reality is pure coincidence.

This book was written using a simple language, respecting the author. The main purpose of this book is to reach everyone in a simple manner and be a blessing, regardless of cultural or spiritual status.

Acknowledgements

I want to Thank each Person That collaborated in one Way or Another to be able to Publish this Book. To Ismael Aranda for Correcting and Translate the Manuscript. To all the team of the Publisher house, for be Kind Patient and Professional. May God bless and Reward you Greatly For your help, Devotion and Dedication. Thank you.

Content

Introduction --------------------------------6

1–A Purpose for Your Life -----------------10

2 – Sowing a Stranger ----------------------19

3 – Dropping Out of School ----------------33

4 – From the Country to the City ----------48

5 – Training Time --------------------------71

6 – Facing the Enemy ---------------------102

7 – The Recovery Phase ------------------134

8 – Keeping a Promise -------------------155

Introduction

The purpose of this book is to highlight the importance of education. There are many consequences that will haunt you for the rest of your life when you drop out of school. The bullying you suffer in school is nothing compared to the humiliation and way people look down on you when you drop out of school. Then, when you're in a work environment and you don't have education, it gets even worse. If you have a dictator as your supervisor, not only will you have to take care of your own assignments, you'll also have to cover for those who are late and leave early and help those who slow down production. You end up having to do the work that nobody wants to do, on a minimum wage, because you're not qualified for any position because you didn't go to school. You see how greed really is, because there's money and power involved. I hope what I'm about to share with you will make you reflect on this. Don't play with your education; it's a discipline that will determine your future. If you've dropped out of school, it's never too late to go back. With perseverance and a lot of effort, you can achieve your goals and change your own world. 1Timothy 4:12 says: *Don't let anyone look down on you because you are young, but set an example for the believers in speech, in conduct, in love, in faith and in purity.* Since the year of 1980, there's been a lot of talk about the rapture. People would say not to buy houses, not to waste time going to college because the rapture was going to take place soon. That affected the youth's mentality negatively. I was young back then and I heard a lot of negative comments from young people. Some of them dropped out of school and started preaching. Others simply didn't care about anything and didn't make plans for their future, because everything was going to end. To this day, almost forty years later, I hear some young people say that they're dropping out of school and not making plans for their future because the world will end soon. Allow me to respectfully tell you that the world is not going to end yet. We still have plenty of earth to go around for a while, at least for several thousand more years. I recommend you read the book <u>Reunited</u>. About our Lord Jesus' second coming. He's coming soon, but it won't be the rapture or the end of the world. The Lord Jesus is coming to build his kingdom here for a thousand years through the church. The Bible describes this as the Millennium. For a thousand years, everyone who loves God and his just will replace the presidents, governors and all the public servants. There will be no evil on earth because the devil will be chained up during that time. So, young people, hurry up and go to school, prepare yourselves, because you will take those jobs. On one occasion when I was praying, voice said to me: "Tell all the young people to prepare themselves, to think big, to plan ahead, to think about their children, grandchildren and great grandchildren; a long, joyful and peaceful life awaits them." It is said that, during the millennium, life expectancy will increase. Some say it will be one hundred and fifty to two hundred years. So, we have a longlife ahead of us. On another occasion, while I was praying, I heard a voice say to me: "Emphasize the importance of studying to young people, so that they can have good jobs and buy everything they want." These messages are what the Lord wants for all his sons. The Lord will give them wisdom and understanding so that they obtain their university degrees to start businesses, family businesses that will allow you to leave an inheritance for your children and your children's children. Just as the Lord says in his word. That means that he wants all his children live abundantly and enjoy the riches of this world. Someone once said: "The war against discrimination is not fought with weapons, but with knowledge, because those who are educated are the ones who rule." Young people, the positions of the president, deputies, mayors, congressmen, representatives and all public servants await you.

Chapter 1

A Purpose For your Life

Isaiah 60:1-2

Arise, shine; for your light has come, and the glory of the Lord is risen upon you.2 For behold, the darkness shall cover the earth, and deep darkness the people: but the Lord will arise over you, and his glory shall be seen upon you.

It is time to stand up, to uplift the gifts that the Lord has given you and be a blessing to others. We are going to enter a new age of the Church and the Lord Jesus will rise in favor of all those who love him.

Sometimes, it's hard for us to believe that our life can have any kind of purpose when all we seem to have are problems and struggles. It seems as if everything is acting against you, bad things always happen to you. Those who are supposed to love you and care for you suddenly hate and despise you for no reason at all.

But throughout the years, you realize that the circumstances that affected you emotionally the most were the ones that helped you mature. It hurts when those who are supposed to love you despise you, but that also helps you to be stronger when the people you dislike hate you.

It doesn't affect you as much, it slides right off, and you understand that they are only looking at the things you lack, just like those who love you. When something marks your life, you learn your lesson when you overcome it. Because, even the worst things are accompanied by a lesson. In some cases, that lesson is to simply not do that again. Someone once said: I learned two thousand ways not to do it. Likewise, defeats are experiences that will make sure you don't go down the same path again. Now, you must use them as a testimony of what not to do and how to take protect yourself from these circumstances in life. The moment negative things start happening, we tend to become blinded and we let ourselves get carried away by our feelings.

When we let ourselves get carried away by feelings, we always focus on what they did to us, because our emotions consume us, and we cannot see beyond that which over whelms us. We are filled with resentment, bitterness, hatred, revenge, we get depressed and no one can find a good purpose in that.

We only have two options: you either let yourself get dragged by what you feel, and you react just like everyone else, doing evil, or you forgive them and try to do the opposite, knowing that the good that you do unto others will always be rewarded. From our personal experience, we all know how difficult the adolescent phase is. Most of us have felt ugly. Your personality becomes explosive, you get irritated very easily, you don't like your name, you don't like your face, and you don't want anyone to look at you or talk to you. You get depressed because there's a pimple on your face. You start a tantrum if someone sits in the chair you like. You want your parents to give you everything, without being disciplined at all.

It's the phase in which you want to have the same rights as adults, but you also want to have the same privileges as children. You want privileges without responsibilities. The adolescent phase is one of the most difficult and dangerous phases for young people.

It's where you notice all the physical changes in your body. Your hormones are out of control; you want to experiment without responsibility. Adolescence is like a lake full of mud and the only way across it is a narrow and fragile bridge. Every single one of us has been there. Many will fall into the mud and they'll run away when they see how dirty they are. Others can't leave by themselves. If that weren't enough, on top of all those physical changes, there's pressure from friends to see who's in control of the group. If you don't do as you're told, they will humiliate you in front of others and laugh at you. Laughing at others isn't good, it's cruel and the victims are badly hurt. As parents, it's our duty to advise our children not to laugh at other people's misfortunes or faults. When I read this verse in the Bible, about prophet Elisha, it moved me.

2 Kings 2:23-24 says:

And he went up from there to Bethel; and as he was going up by the road, some youths came from the city, and mocked him, and said to him, "Go up, you baldhead! Go up, you baldhead!" So, he turned around and looked them, and pronounced a curse on them, in the name of the Lord. And two female bears came out of the woos and mauled forty-two of the youths.

This really impressed me; those boys were making fun of the prophet Elisha, because he was baldhead. The bible said; some youths, it means that they were not children, maybe they were teenagers. If the bears tore forty-two of them apart, that means there were more of them. Perhaps they had just dropped out of school. Can you imagine forty-two families crying out for their youths?

The prophet Elisha was going through a very difficult situation. He had just lost his mentor, his spiritual father, the prophet Elijah. He couldn't stand being mocked by the boys. He cursed them, in Jehovah's name, and God sent two bears to kill them for having laughed at the prophet Elisha.

That also means that bullying, humiliating others, will not go unpunished. If you don't know what's going through their mind or what they're going through, and you've offended them, and they cry out to God, your life could be destroyed, and it will affect your entire family.

Here's a great piece of advice from the apostle Paul, so that you're not influenced by those who do evil unto others,

1 Timothy 6:5 says:

Useless wrangling of men of corrupt minds, and destitute of the truth, suppose that godliness is a means of gain. From such withdraw yourself.

It seems like the apostle Paul also had to make big decisions during his youth. A true friend will never ask you to do something that affects or compromises your integrity. True friendship is measured by respect, towards you and your family.

If a friend does not respect your family, they do not respect you either and that also applies to your significant other. Walk with integrity, according to the motivations and reasons of your conviction, to achieve your goals. Doors to new opportunities will open for a better future.

God's purpose for your life:

All this is much easier when you invite the Lord Jesus to dwell in your heart. May he guide and direct you according to his will.

> 2 Corinthians 5:17 says:

Therefore, if anyone is in Christ, he is a new creature: old things have passed away; behold, all things have become new.

He has great plans and wonderful purposes for your life. Therefore, he wants you to mature and bring out the best in you from the mistakes and defeats that have wanted to paralyze you. Ask God to transform your heart and mind. When God changes your heart, you have control over yourself, your feelings and emotions, and you approach everything differently.

You don't allow yourself to be carried away by what you feel, but by the reason of your convictions. God prepared a perfect plan for humanity.

As John 3: 16–17 says:

For God so loved the world, that He gave His only begotten Son, that whoever believeth in Him should not perish, but have everlasting life. For God did not send His Son into the world to condemn the world; but that the world through Him might be saved.

All we need to do is acknowledge the sacrifice He made on the cross of Calvary and accept Him as our Lord and Savior. It's that simple and that easy. We can all achieve it, in our Lord Jesus' name.

Chapter 2

Sowing A Stranger

Proverbs 15:3

The eyes of the Lord are in every place, keeping watch on the evil and the good.

I want to share some experiences that weren't so good during my childhood and adolescence, when I thought that my life had no purpose. I was born in Mexico, in a very small rural community located in one of the most remote mountains. There were no public services and the nearest town was almost three hours away. There were only around twelve or fifteen families that lived there. We made a living by harvesting the crops we sowed every season.

A Stranger

When I was eight years old, one of the girls from the ranch married a man from another town. When the sowing season began, no one wanted to rent him a child to help him could sow, because he was a stranger.

The man was so desperate that he went to all the families and offered to pay them twice as much. And since I had already learned how to sow with my father the year before, my mother decided that I should work with him. She told the man that she was going to trust him and lend him one of her girls. He was very happy; he said he would greatly appreciate it. My mom said that, meanwhile, my dad would continue teaching my younger siblings, so they could also rent one of them if someone needed help. The man's father-in-law lent him the lands that were at the foot of the hill. When the mountains look blue, it's due to the distance; that means that it is very far away. He picked me up very early; everything was still very dark, and all my brothers were asleep.

We used sandals that my dad made us, but our feet got wet and they hurt a lot due to the morning dew on the plants. We didn't have jackets, we just wore another shirt, but it felt very cold in the morning. That man had male oxen; those are the strongest animals to work with, but also the hardest to tame.

He rides on one of the males and he'd put me another one's saddle, tie me very tight with a rope, and he would guide that animal. In addition to that, he would carry everything he needed for work: sacks with tools, seeds, food and water. Along the way, we went through different fields where other men also worked. He would always stop at one field where one of his brothers-in-law worked to greet him. This man had very naughty children. They told me that, in the big mountains, where their grandpa's lands were, there were lions, bears and snakes so big that they ate cows. I believed everything they said, and I was very scared.

I was so afraid of getting eaten by the giant snakes that I would not use the bathroom; I would wait until I got home so I could use the bathroom. Every time he stopped to talk with his brother-in-law, the children would tell me scary stories. And as we were leaving, those little boys would poke the animal's stomach with a stick and that would make him kick with all its strength.

It scared me a lot. Everything I had hanging on the saddle, the water jugs that were made of iron, the sacks with tools hit my feet very hard and I started crying as they all laughed. On top of that, from the first day we started working, the man gave me two crossed backpacks full of corn, so I could sow with both hands. I told him that I couldn't do that, I only knew how to sow with one backpack.

He told me I was going to learn there, because he had to sow all his lands in two weeks. He hit the males and they ran. He told me that, if I didn't come sowing right behind him, he would place me in front of the animals and if I didn't run as I was sowing, he would let them step on me. I was very afraid of those animals because, when he hit them, not even he could control them.

So, I had to run all day, sowing with both hands. I got very tired, the backpacks felt very heavy. In addition to that, the ties grazed both sides of my neck. I was not used to working like that. I was only eight years old and they were barely teaching me how to work in the fields. I had only sowed once with my dad's donkeys.

It felt like they worked in slow motion and he let me sleep for a while, so I could rest. But with this man, it was quite the opposite. When I told him that my father didn't make me do that, he replied that he wasn't my dad, that he was paying a lot of money for my work and I had to do it. When we got to his house, his wife served us dinner, but I had a stomach achebecause I wanted to go to the bathroom. I asked him to let me take my food home and I would eat it there because I wanted to go. The man said he was not going to take me home until I finished my meal, but I couldn't eat, and I would start crying.

His wife told him to take me as soon as he finished eating, but he got upset because I didn't eat; he took my plate and gave it to the dogs. I told him not to throw my food away, I was very hungry, but I wanted to take it to my house, but he was upset and would not let me take it home.

When he took me home, all my brothers were already asleep, only my dad was there waiting for me. But there was no food for me there, because the man was supposed to feed me. I would only eat the lunch we had at noon in the fields. The first day we came back, my dad asked me if the man had treated me well. When I told him what the naughty kids did to me, my dad got very upset. The next day, when the man went to pick me up, my dad told him that I had told him everything that happened. He told him that he had agreed to go work with him because of the situation he was going through, since no one wanted to lend him any of their children. So, he expected him to take care of me, because if he didn't calm those naughty children, I wouldn't work with him anymore.

He said he apologized and that it wouldn't happen again. Well, I was feeling better, thinking that this man was going to defend me, but when we ran into the naughty children, they did the same thing, everyone laughed at me and he didn't say anything to them. When we arrived at the planting fields, the man was very angry at me.

He told me that everything the children said was true. He said that if I told my dad anything again, he would leave me tied up on a tree while he finished sowing. He said that later hewould tie me down on the ground, so the giant animals could eat me, and I would never see my dad again.He said he would tell my dad that I had gone to the bathroom, gotten lost and eaten by some animals in the hill and that my dad would never see me again. I was even more afraid, and I was terrified of that man. Those two weeks were the worst moments of my life.He didn't even try to stop those children, because he didn't get along with his brother-in-law.

So, it was easier to threaten me, so that I would stay quiet and not tell my dad anything. When we got home, my father asked me how the children had behaved, if the man had calmed them down. I said they had behaved well, but it wasn't true. The same thing happened every day.

From that moment, I was as afraid of that man as I was of the giant animals. Every day, I thought that, when I finished working, I wouldn't make it back home. I cried all the way every day, thinking that maybe I wouldn't make it back to see my dad. When we had finished sowing, I told my dad everything that man had said to me. My dad was very upset, he told my mom that she was never going to make any decision regarding me again without his consent. He assured me that he was going to see to it that I would never work with a stranger again. About four months after that, my mom went to buy something from the store with the naughty children's mother.

When she got back, she was very happy. She said that the lady wanted to hire me, to sow for her husband the following year. Everyone was very surprised that they lent these lands to the son-in-law, because they were very far away, and they weren't good for planting crops.

They didn't know what happened to these lands, since theyhad the best harvest of any of the nearby fields. All the cornfield was distributed evenly, as if it had been measured. In addition, all the furrows were sown from shore to shore and well laden with corn. Their harvest was all lost and they didn't understand why, since the other lands weren't good. They wanted to see if my hand was blessed. My mom asked herif she knew what her children did to me. She said that they told her that they liked playing with me. My mom said that I told her quite the opposite. She insisted that she'd paid us whatever we wanted, and they would lend us one of their children to help my dad sow.

In addition to that, she would send one of her girls so that I wouldn't be alone with the other children and her husband in the fields. My mom told my dad and he got very upset. He said that he wouldn't let me go with those people for all the gold in the world. A few days later, my mom sent me some of my younger siblings to buy something from that lady's store.

(I think it was on purpose, to convince me to go to work with them). The lady told her children, they asked me for forgiveness and her husband also apologized. She told me to take anything I wanted from her store: toys, dolls or candy. Anything I wanted, she wouldlet me have it. I said I didn't want anything, I only asked her for what my mother had asked me to get from the store. She told me that, whenever I wanted, I could go and play with her daughters and she would let me keep all the toys or dolls that I liked. I told her that I already had a lot of brothers that I could play with at home and we didn't need anything.

My little brothers told my mom and my other siblings everything. (My mother was very smart, whenever she sent us out on some errand, she sent two of us, she sent someone who was quiet and someone who was talkative, who usually didn't get along with each other, so that they would tattle on each other and tell her everything that happened.)

My brothers told me not to be dumb, to gowork with them because they were going to pay my mom a lot of money and they were going to give me anything I wanted from their store, but I couldn't get over that. I was very afraid and full of anger and resentment. I did not want to see them, let alone work with them.Since the community was small, it seems like everyone found out about what the lady had said. When we went down to the river to get water for the animals, the gentlemen asked my dad if I was the child with the blessed hand. Since my dadwas also offended, he exaggerated a bit.

He would tell them: "Yes, she is, you can always see how she does things differently." They would say: "Well, let me rent her, just to try and see if that's true. I'll pay youwhatever youwant." And he answered: "No, I don't have to prove anything to anyone. I know what I have, and I won't let me daughter go again, not for all the gold in the world. Those scoundrels mistreated her and didn't even feed her."

20 years after I gave myself to the Lord, when I was forty years old. Every time I remembered that, something troubled me with the Lord. Ididn't understand why he had blessed that man with such a good harvest. He saw everything they did to me. I

was only a girl and I didn't know how to defend myself. It was something my mind couldn't comprehend. Until one day, as I was praying, I asked the Lord: "Lord, to this day, I still can't understand why. If you are a just God and you saw what all that those people did to me, why did you bless that man with such a good harvest?"

The Lord answered: "So that they would regret everything they did to you." Those words went straight to my heart and my eyes were opened. It came to my mind, like an image, and I saw everything that lady did, so I would go work with them. That's when I started to cry, thanking God and I asking for forgiveness.

For so many years, I resented these people and then God, because it was unfair. But it had never occurred to me that I should ask him why he did it. Sometimes, we are so hurt by resentment that we don't realize what God is doing for us. He immediately did justice and blessed the work of my hands. They lost their harvest and it made them regret everything they did. I never saw that stranger again. My father said that people told him that whenever he heard that we were going to the river with our animals, the man would quickly go somewhere else. My dad was very calm, he didn't like confronting anyone, but since all the locals found out, I think he also felt very bad and couldn't see my dad eye to eye.

When people repent with all their heart, they always try to correct their mistakes. And that is what God wants us to do; no matter how much evil we've done, we need todo good, so we can find his grace and mercy. By doing so, when we find ourselves in difficult situations, we can cry out to him for help. God is always faithful and does justice, but on many occasions we don't realize that he's doing so.

Chapter 3

Dropping Out of School

Proverbs 1: 8-9

My sonhear the instruction of your father, and do not forsake the law of your mother; For they will be gracefulornament on your head, and chains about your neck.

When I was thirteen, I didn't want to go back to school because I couldn't stand the children teasing me because everyone had gone to the next grade, while I failed. I never imagined the consequences of that bad decision. I didn't see the children at school anymore, so they wouldn't bully me. But I had ten brothers at home, so jokes, ridicule, scolding and punishment were part of my daily routine for having dropped out of school. At school, it was only for a little while, but at home it was from sunrise to sunset, seven days a week.

And if that weren't enough, after doing my own assignments, I always ended up doing my brothers' assignments because they said that they had homework and I didn't. My mother said that it was fine, that I had to do it as punishment for having dropped out of school.

When I was eleven years old, I had to sow for my older brother and he taught me to work with the plow on horseback, which usually worked with. I liked working with him because he was very patient. He didn't scold us when we were wrong, on the contrary, he encouraged us to do better next time. The following year, he told me to help my dad, so I could get some practice with thedonkeys, because those were slower. It was very different with the donkeys because, since they were slower, it was easier for me. Eventually, I guided the oxen and my dad sowed for me.

Well, continuing with the story: Something that affected me a lot when I left school was one day when I got back home from working in the field and I was very tire. I threw myself on the bedroll to rest. Suddenly, one of my sisters came running to tell me to go outside, because my godmother was visiting and wanted to see me.

When you think of a godmother, the first thing that comes to your mind is someone who loves you very much and when she visits and asks about you, she'll brings you candy at least. So, I got up quickly and ran to see my godmother. When I got to the patio, there was aline of girls next to my little sisters who had graduated from elementary school.

They all had their diploma in their hands and they were showing it to me. They looked so pretty, with new dresses, new shoes, very well combed, all smiling. Then my godmother told me: "I brought them here, so you could see that they have already graduated from school.

Since you dropped out of school, you're going to be dumb, working in the field all the time, like animals." She said: "Just look at yourself." I looked at myself and I was wearing my sandals and all my clothes were ripped and very dirty. I couldn't say anything, I just ran away, crying and went to the corrals to hide among the hay.

When my father arrived (he had gone to the river with my brothers to give the animals water), my little sisters told him everything and he got very upset. He told my mom that she should not have allowed me to be humiliated like that. She said she allowed it, so that I would regret having dropped out of school.

That affected me a lot and I started to feel hatred and anger towards everyone. No body looked at the hard work I did. I worked in the field all day, just as much as my father and my brothers. Also, I had to do my chores at home. On Saturdays, we took all the clothes down to the river in sacks, so we could wash them.

We spent all day there, washing, drying and folding clothes. My mother sent us something to eat. On Sundays, we did general cleaning and we also brought buckets of water from the well for the plants and house. I had very thick calluson my hands that I would cut off with knives, because when they grew a lot and hurt.

But I guess no one was saw that and on top of that they ridiculed and scornedme, even the people who you'd least expect. Then, my two older brothers went to work in the city. We sold the two males and only kept the two female oxen. I took the horses and my dad took the donkeys.

That same year, my older sister also left the ranch to work with some ladies in Laredo, Texas. That affected me a lot. At that moment, I was the oldest and I had my seven younger siblings. I was a teenager; everyone was keeping an eye on the boys. I couldn't even think about that, because no one would notice me.

I felt very ugly and, in addition to that, I always walked around with dirty and ripped clothes. We passed our clothes down to one another, but my mom kept my older sister's clothes in a padlocked suitcase for my younger siblings. She said that I didn't need it and she told me to use my dad and brothers' old clothes, so that was what I used.

I cut my dad's oldest pants and tied them with a thin lasso. When I was sixteen, I started getting very sick. The work was too heavy, and the food was not very good. On top of that, I didn't like milk or warm eggs; that was what my mom reserved for my dad and brothers during the work season. I preferred beans with potato tacos and roasted chili peppers. My skin was stuck to my bones and I had a lot of white spots everywhere. Then, when the sun came up, I got a very strong headache that felt like my head was going to explode. I didn't want to stop the oxen, because we had to stay later anyway, until the day ended.

But then, my nose started bleeding a lot. My dad would cover my nose and blood would come out through my mouth. He would put all the water we had to drink on my head and set me under a shadow until it passed. That's when I started to feel even worse. I was very depressed.

Firstly, because my sister left, she was the one I talked to the most, and secondly, because I had no other choice. I didn't think about any future, I felt like I was one of the animals who worked in the field. The only thing that help me together was being able to help my dad, because of the great love he had for me and I didn't want to fail him. Since I couldn't work anymore, I felt like I was no longer useful, and I didn't want to be a burden for him. I tried to take my own life several times. Whenever I heard that something was poisonous, I ran and tried using it, but nothing worked. I caught the most poisonous scorpions and put them on my hand, so they would sting me, but they didn't have any effect on me.

It made me very angry and I started crying. It was so frustrating that I couldn't kill myself with anything, so one day, after a very bad headache, I asked my dad for permission to go home. He said yes, but I went and hid until they left. Then, I went to a hill, because it had a very big boulder and I was going to jump from there.

I walked along the hill and it seemed very low. I thought: "If I jump from here, I'm not going to kill myself. If anything, I'll break my hand or leg. Also, it's going to get dark and nobody will walk by, so the coyotes will eat me alive." That scared me. I walked all around and there was no place high enough for me to jump off.

I went back to the middle of the fallow. The cornfields were up to my knees. I looked at the sky, everything was completely blue, there wasn't a single cloud, and the sun had already set. I felt so desperate that I started screaming with all my might.

(At that time, my older sister had already told me about the Lord, but I didn't want to accept him because I didn't believe in him.) I shouted: "God, if you are as real as my sister says, send a lightning bolt and kill me. I don't want to live anymore, get me out of here, because I can't take it anymore." I screamed until I got tired.

Then, I fell to my knees, in the middle of the furrow in the cornfields, I covered my face with both of my hands and started crying loudly. As I was crying, with my hands still covering my face, I felt something like a reflection of light. I quickly uncovered my face and there was a very large, thick and white cloud in the sky. The sun was still lighting up that cloud. It really shocked me, and I thought: "Where did that cloud come from? I had just looked up at the sky and there was nothing." I was shaking, simply watching. Then, the cloud began to spin a little and three thick rays of white light began to descend from the center of the cloud with the sunlight's reflection.

The rays began to descend slowly, which is not normal. I quickly started thinking and said: "What did I do? I provoked the wrath of God and now he is going to burn me with those rays of light." I got up quickly and started running towardsmy house. I ran down the mountain as fast as I could, and I could feel the fire on my back.

As I was arriving to my house, I had to jump a tall fence and I thought that the light would catch up to me there. I started yelling at my dad and my little brothers with all my strength. I wanted them to see me, where I was, before the cloud burned me, because then nobody would recognize me. They all ran outside, thinking I was being chased by some animal.

They shouted at me: "What's wrong with you? What's going on?" I yelled back: "Look at the cloud! Look at the cloud!" I didn't want to look at it, because I thought that all his anger would be unleashed if I did. They all said: "What cloud? What are you talking about?"

When I looked up at the sky, there was no cloud; the sky was completely blue. Everyone started laughing and said: "What are you talking about? Where's the cloud?" I tried to play it cool, so that they wouldn't laugh at me, and I said: "Haha, you fell for it! It was so you would come outside to greet me." They said: "You're crazy," and they all ran back inside.

I ran after them and I went to bed without eating dinner. I was shaking, but how could I tell them? Nobody would believe me. The next day, I asked my father if he would let us go walk around the cornfields where I had seen the cloud the day before. I wanted to go see the place, I thought that at least the field would have burned.

I went there and there was no sign of anything. I didn't comment on any of that again, because nobody would believe me. It was until several years when my older sister went back to the city that I told her about it and she did believe me. She said: "The three rays of light that you saw represent the Father, the Son and the Holy Spirit.

The Lord appeared before you in that cloud and he was going to talk to you there." I said: "What was he going to say?" She answered: "Well, I do not know. Why did you run?" I said: "It's just that I thought the light was going to burn me." She said: "Didn't you want to die? Why didn't you wait?"

I said: "I wanted to die, but I wanted to get hit by lightning so that it would be instant. I didn't want to be burned alive, that was very gruesome." She started laughing. Then, she told the pastor and he also laughed. He said: "Come on, my sister, Rosita, if you wanted to die, why didn't you wait?" I said: "Well, yes, I wanted to die, but in a different way. I wanted something instant, not so gruesome." Well, going back to the story: The following week after that experience, my mother thought about going to visit my grandmother in the city, because she needed clothes for the children. Which was not very common, since she only went around Christmas time and it was the beginning of August.

My dad told her she could go and to take me along, so I could see a doctor, because I was very sick. My mom took me to a pharmacy in the city where there were always doctors available. The doctor said I had severe anemia and prescribed some vitamins, but above all,I had to eat very healthy.A lady named Carmen told my mom to let me to work with her, because she needed a girl.

She told her that my dad wouldn't allow that, because it was the work season. The lady gave us her phone number in case they decided to let me go, so they could call her, and she'd pick me up. When we returned, my mom told my dad and he said that he would rather have me far away if I was fine, because if I stayed and helped him, I was most likely going to die. So then, my mom went to the nearest town and spoke to Mrs. Carmen by phone. She told her that they would pick me up next week. I started wondering if God had heard me and he was going to get me out of there.

But I didn't say anything, I just kept everything to myself. That same week that they were going to pick me up, my dad gave me a lot of advice. He said that I should be very careful, that I should never take what's not mine, because everything belongs to someone who has workedhard to pay for that.

If I ever found money on the ground, I should find who it belongs to, because rich people do that to test you, but if you leave it there, someone else will take it and they'll blame you. I should never leave a job without letting them know; no matter how badly they treated me, I should let them know that they should look for someone else. He told me that, in the meantime, I should work the best I can, never be late, finish all my assignments. I should help my fellow coworkers so that, when I leave, they will miss me and regret what they did to me. I should always try to leave with my head held high, on good terms, because you don't know if you might go back to that place someday.

He said: "If you don't like your work, you should look for another job before talking bad about your current job. Because no one should talk bad about their sour of income, because it's like cursing yourself." He told me to be very careful with old people, they shouldn't be disrespected.

That I should help them whenever I had the opportunity, because whatever you do to an old man, someone will do the same to you one day. We're all headed in the same direction and maybe you'll never see that old man again, but if you did something for him, whether it's good or bad, someone else will also do that for you. I always tried to follow his advice and believe me, it works.

Chapter 4

From the Country to The City

Psalm 37: 23-24

The steps of a good man are ordered by the Lord: and he delighteth in his way. Though he fall, he shall not be utterly cast down: for the Lord upholds him with His hand.

When Mrs. Carmen picked me up at the ranch to take me to work in the city, I asked her how much she was going to me pay per week in front of my parents. I wanted to send them money, so they could pay someone to help my dad finish his harvest. She said $120.00 pesos per week. We thought it was good, since in the countryside they paid us $90.00 pesos. As I was on my way to the city, I had a lot of dreams. I wanted to send them as much as I could to help my parents and buy things for my little brothers.

The lady had a store in a shopping mall and a small sewing workshop in her house. At the workshop, they would only cut all the fabric for the sheets and bedspread sets. Her husband brought the fabrics to the seamstresses who worked at their house. The lady told me that I was going to take care of her four children and the chores around the house.

I would also help her husband cut the fabric and steam iron all the sheets and covers they collected from the seamstresses. I steam-ironed 40 to 50 sets of sheets every day, on my knees, in the store, behind the counters. I placed them in bags, separated them by size and then stored them in the warehouse that was on the second floor. I also helped by cleaning the store and supplying everything that the store needed. On Sundays, she left me at home with the children and she would leave all the dirty clothes out for me to wash.

She had a washing machine that only washed, it didn't dry. I finished washing the clothes in the laundry room and then I set it out to dry on the clotheslines. I folded the clothes that was dry and kept in their drawers to avoid having to iron it later. They also brought me everything I needed to make dinner for them.

One day, I asked the lady if they could bring me a workshop table to the store, one of the tables they didn't use, so that I could iron there, because my back and knees were tired. She said no, because if they started giving me those kinds of commodities, I was going to get used to that. She said I should thank God that I didn't have to walk in the sun like animals anymore, at least now I worked in the shade. At the end of my first week, I asked her if I she would please send my mom the money, so that they could pay whoever was helping my dad. She told me that first, I needed to buy clothes, because the clothes I had was not suitable for walking around the city, she would buy it for me and deduct it from my salary.

I asked my dad if he would let me take his Sunday clothes and I'd buy him some more. He said yes, I could take whatever I wanted. So, I took my dad's best clothes. I told the lady that they were waiting on the money to pay someone else. She said that she didn't know my parents' address.

I told her that my mom assured me that she knew how to send letters and she replied that she didn't know how to do that and that, if I didn't want clothes as payment, then she would save the money until my mom came in December. I felt very bad and desperate. It was the last week of August, it was still a long time until December and my dad needed that money. I realized that wasn't going to work, because that wasn't our agreement. I didn't know what to do; I didn't know how to communicate with my parents, so I couldtell them that I wanted to go back and help my dad. It was very exasperating; I felt trapped and didn't know how to go back home.

I seriously started regretting not having gone to school. The lady told me she didn't want me to talk to anyone, with clients or workers from other stores. So, when someone asked me something, I didn't answer. On one occasion, I went to the cafeteria to ask the lady if she could warm the bottles for the children.

There were some girls and a boy who worked at the stores on either side. Whenever I walked by where they worked, they would talk to me, but I didn't reply. They said: "Look at the mute kid's eyes. Hey, what kind of drugs are you on?" And everyone in the cafeteria started laughing. The lady in the cafeteria asked me: "Girl, what's the matter with you? Whenever you come here, your eyes are very red. Do you cry a lot?" I replied: "No. The thing is, I iron 40 to 50 sets of sheets on the floor every day and all of the steam gets in my face. That's why my eyes are red." She told the others: "Did you guys hear why her eyes are red?"

She told them about it and she asked them not to laugh at me. She said that she would like to see them do what I did. They never said anything to me again. So, the months went by and my older brother arrived in November, when he went to see my parents at the ranch.

My dad cried, because he never expected that from me, that I hadleft, and I never thought about them. I told him what was going on and told him to take me with him. He said he would, but I had to ask the lady for the money since he only had enough for his ticket. My parents thought that I was saving the money and they expected me to send something with him. I asked Mrs.

Carmen if she could give me the money, because I wanted to send it with my brother. She said that, since he arrived unannounced, she didn't have the money and that she would keep saving it for me until my mother came in December. My brother also got upset and had to go back without any money.

I was very desperate and crying. I wanted to hit myself against a wall. Why didn't I go to school? Why didn't I even learn to read so I could write them and tell them what was happening to me? Since my brother told my mom what was going on, she decided that she wouldn't risk going for me without any money.

Instead, she would wait for my older sister to visit in February, to see if she would lend her money for both of our passages. When my mom arrived on the last week of February, I was ironing in the back. I heard the children shout that my mom had arrived. I hid behind the sheets that were on display to hear what the lady was saying to her.

After greeting her, she told her that she had bad news. She said that unfortunately I couldn't read or write and that I didn't help her at all. She said they couldn't pay me because sales weren't good and all they could only give us was enough for the ticket, so she could take me back home.

When I heard that, I felt very bad. It was so much infuriating that I quickly ran out and said: "You're an evil woman! You always said you were saving my money for me and now you come up with this story." My mother told me: "Don't be disrespectful." I ran, crying, I ran around the entire mall. I wanted to run to the mountains, so I could cry and get it all out, but there was nowhere to hide.

I sat on a bench next to some small trees, I covered my face with my hands and cried there. When I uncovered my face, I was surrounded by the girls and the boy who laughed at me, but they were all very serious. One of the girls said to me: "Is the lady who just arrived your mother?" I just shook my head and said yes. She asked: "Did she come to pick you up?" I said yes again. She said: "And you don't want to leave, right?" I replied: "Yes, I want to leave. I can't take it anymore. The problem is that the lady always told me she was saving my money, but now she told my mother that she's not going to pay me, because I'm not good at anything."

They took me to a store and gave me water, so I would calm down a bit. They told me to take my mom, so she could sue her; they said they would be witnessesof how she had me as a slave. When I calmed down, I went to get my mom. I told herthat we should go for a walk, so she could get to know the place.

The lady told me: "Before you leave, clean up that mess you have back there." I replied: "Well, you're going to have to do it yourself, because I'm not good at doing anything." My mom told her that I would clean up when we got back. I took her to the girls and they explained everything and how she could sue her. But my mother said no, she didn'thave the time or money for that. Then they told her to leave me with someone and they were going help me find a job where they would pay me. My mother told them that the problem was that, if she left me, she couldn't come back for me, because there was no way of getting the money for the tickets to the ranch.

They insisted that she leave me for two months and if I still didn't have a job when she returned, they would all help pay for both of our tickets. I begged my mom to leave me, I really wanted to work, because I couldn't help my dad in the fields anyway. My mother told them she was going to see where she could leave me, because she had to go back to the ranch the next day.

My mom always went to my grandma's house. When we arrived, I asked her for permission to stay at her house, because I wanted to keep working. She said that she couldn't be held responsible for anyone and it would be very difficult for me to find a job in the city since I didn't know how to read or write. She said I should just go back and help my dad in the field in any way I could. At night, before going to bed, I said: "God, could you do a miracle and find me a place to stay?" As I was falling asleep, I remembered a lady who went to the store one day who had invited me to her house whenever I had a day off.

I told her I didn't have any days off. She replied that I should have a day off and she wrote down her address. She said that all I had to do was grab a taxi, give the driver the little piece of paper and he would take me there. She said she'd take me back to work. But I never built up the courage to do that.

First, I didn't have any money to pay for a taxi, and second, I didn't know my way around the city and if I got lost, I couldn't read the streets. So, I just kept that piece of paper. I quickly got up and looked inside the box where I had my things and pulled out that little piece of paper. Since my mom was already asleep, I didn't tell her anything. I couldn't sleep that night since I was thinking so much, and I fell asleep in the morning. My mother woke me up, it was getting late because we had to take the bus at eight in the morning. I quickly got up and, since my grandmother was there, I couldn't tell my mom anything.

As soon as we went outside, a taxi drove by and my mother asked the driver to take us to the bus terminal. She got in the taxi and the man opened the trunk for me, so I could store my things. I asked the taxi driver if he could take us to that address first, because I wanted to say goodbye to someone. He said yes.

When the taxi driver stopped, my mother said: "What's going on? This isn't the bus terminal." He said: "That's the address your daughter gave me." I said: "I just want to say goodbye to a lady who treated me very well." She said: "Well, hurry up." She stayed in the taxi. I knocked on the door and no one opened. I grabbed a rock and I started knocking very hard. The lady came out in her nightgown. I said: "Do you remember me?" She said: "No, who are you?" I desperately said: "I'm the girl from the store, you invited me to your house and gave me your address on a piece of paper." She said: "Oh, yes, now I remember. Come in." I said: "The thing is, my mom came to take me home, but I don't want to leave because I want to keep working, but I don't have anywhere to stay.

Would you happen to have space for me?" She replied: "Of course, we have space for you here. Tell your mom to come in, we'll take her to the center bus in a little while." My mom said: "But I don't know that lady." I replied: "But she's letting me stay at her house and she seems like a good person.

Come so you can meet her, and you don't feel comfortable, then we'll go to the terminal." My mom answered: "Well, you're right, let me talk to her first." We got our things out, paid the taxi and went inside the house. The lady told my mother to leave me for two months, that I would help her at home and with her children in the meantime. If I still didn't have a job when she came back, she would pay me something for having helped her. After lunch, I went to drop my mother off at the bus terminal, so that she could take the twelve o'clock bus.

Mrs. Sofia told me not to be afraid of walkingon the street, all I had to do was show a taxi driver the paper and she would pay him when I got home. My mom left me the money for the bus ticket,so I could pay for the taxis until I learned how to take the bus. She also told me to help the lady in any way I could, so that I would grab my food.

From the plant, I took a taxi and went to the shops of the mall to tell the girls that I had stayed, so they could find me a job soon. They were all very happy. They said that they were going to get me a job there and they were going to teach me how to read and write. They told me to come back in two days to find out what the owner of the store where they worked at had decided. We agreed on that and I went back to Mrs.

Sofia's house. Meanwhile,I tried to help her as much as I could, I did the cleaning around the house, swept the sidewalk. Since I was used to going to bed early, I got up early. The lady had the dirty laundry in the ironing room. I washed her clothes and made breakfast for her and her children.

When the lady woke up, she said: "You don't have to do this, because you're going to get us used to it and then you'll start working." I would say: "Well, in the meantime, take advantage of it, teach me new recipes and I'll teach you some recipes we cooked in the ranch." And that's what we did when I wasn't working.

When I went back to the mall, I was just walking in through the main entrance, when suddenly one of the girls came and took me to another store. Then the others arrived and told me that the day I went to tell them I was staying; the boy had thought about going to tell Mrs. Carmen, the lady I worked with before, that they would find me a job where they would pay me. The next day, when the owner arrived, Mrs. Carmen spoke to him and took him to her store. When he came back, he was very upset. He told them that the lady had told him that his employees wanted to lie to him, so a girl could work at his store. But that girl wasn't good at anything; she couldn't read or write and when she was working with her, she lost a lot of money.

The owner was very angry and warned them that if he ever saw this girl step foot in his store, he would fire all of them. They asked me not to come back, because I was going to get them in trouble. They told me to call them next Saturday, but they were thinking that it would be better for me to try to get a job at a factory in the city center.

I told them it was fine, that I didn't want to get them in trouble. I was very grateful for everything they were doing for me. I went back to the house, crying. I never stole a single cent from that lady and I thought that everything was over at that point. When I told Mrs. Sofia, she told me not to worry, there were many jobs everywhere and she was also going to help me find a job. I felt very bad and regretted having dropped out of school as a child. I cried and wanted to hit myself against the floor. How could I have wasted those important years of my childhood? Now that I understood, I realized that no one was going to give me a job in the city if I didn't know how to read or write.

A week later, the following Saturday, I was afraid to call them, because I didn't want to hear bad news. I thought that if the lady had learned that I was there, she could have let the other owner know, just to hurt the girls. When I called her, the girl said: "We have a job for you." I said: "Really? Where?"

She said: "Right here, at the mall." I replied: "But that won't work, because if the lady has already done it with one owner, she'll do it with the others. She's going to say bad things about me." The girl answered, saying: "Don't worry, that's not going to happen anymore because we told Mrs. Silvia, the owner of another store, everything and she said: 'Bring me that girl. I'm going to give her a job.' She said that you should come here tomorrow, Sunday, so you can talk to her husband." I couldn't believe it. I told them I would be there, and I thanked them. I told Mrs. Sofia, and she was also very happy. The next day, when I arrived, the girls took me to another store.

One of them brought me some high-heels, another girl lent me a skirt and another one lent me a blouse. After changing my clothes, they released my braids, combed my hair and put some makeup on me so I would be ready for the job interview. Then, they took me to the other owner's shop for the interview and left me there by myself.

The man's name was Raul and he asked me why I wanted to work. I told him I just wanted to work to get some money that I could send to my dad, so he could pay someone to help him pick his crop. He replied: "Look girl, your intentions to help your dad are very good, but first of all, you have to get that mentality out of your head."

He said: "You will have lots of opportunities here and you can grow as much as you want. You can be an ordinary employee. If you try harder, you can be one of the best employees. And depending on how good you are with math, you could become a cashier or perhaps even a manager at one of my businesses."

I laughed and said: "No sir, I don't think I aspire to that much." He said: "Well it's all up to you. But pay close attention to me, I'm going to give you some advice that will help you be successful for the rest of your life, if you live by it." That impressed me, and I decided to pay close attention. He said: "Never work only for money, because money is spent faster than you imagine.

First: Work for knowledge; learn everything you can in every area. Knowledge will stay with you and it's what will bring you new opportunities wherever you go. Because whenever you go and look for work, they'll always ask you what you can do. Second: Work to provide a service for others.

Whatever you do, believe that you're doing something that will benefit others. When you work and try to help others, your big boss on heaven will be happy because He likes when someone is doing good unto others. And third: Work for money, because money is what will help you pay for all your expenses.

Believe me, if you do it in this order, you will always succeed in life." I thanked him for his advice. He told me that he had professional girls at the store downtown and that they would teach me everything I needed to know. He told me to show up the next day to start my training.

He said that they were going to test me for two months and if I worked hard and learned the basics during that time, he would give me the opportunity to start working there, if I promised to go to school in the afternoon to improve myself. It's very difficult to face life without having studied. Education is the means that prepare us for the work environment. He said: "Right now, you're realizing how difficult it is to face life without having studied." I told him that he was right; I was paying dearly for not having gone to school. He said that, during my trial, they were only going to pay me a little bit. Once I passed the trial, they would pay me the same as the others, $750.00 pesos. I asked him: "Is that per month?"

He replied: "No, per week. That's the minimum wage here." I couldn't believe it. In the fields, we worked under the sun all day and we only got paid 90 pesos per week. He said: "But during these first two months, we're only going to pay you 450." That alone surprised me.

The other lady said that she was going to pay me 120, but in the end, shedidn't pay me anything after six months of work. I wanted to scream and jump with excitement, but I was very quiet. He gave me the address on a piece of paper and said he would be waiting for me at 9 in the morning. As I was leaving, he said: "Wait, who lentyou those shoes?" (He realized I had never worn heels in my life) I replied: "The girls brought me these clothes and the shoes for the interview." He said: "You have very good friends. However, you should wear comfortable clothes tomorrow, because the work is very tiring, and I don't think you'll be able to put up with those shoes all day."

I said: "It's just that my clothes are the ones I used in the field. Is it okay if I wear that?" Here plied: "Don't worry, just wear something comfortable." Iwent and told the girls the news; they were all very happy. I thanked them for everything they did for me and I promised them that, when I had a day off, I would visit them and tell them everything.

Mrs. Sofia was also very happy and said that she was going to take me on my first day of work, so she could show me the way and where I had to take the buses. I barely slept because I was so happy. I finally had a job and they were going to teach me how to read and write. Also, I thought about the advice that the gentleman gave me, so that I wouldn't forget it. Well, we'll continue in the next chapter.

Chapter 5

Training Time

Psalm 37: 5-6

Commit thy way to the Lord; trust also in Him; He shall bring it to pass. And He shall bring forth you righteousness as the light, and your justice as the noonday.

Well, my first day of work arrived. I got up very early, I took a shower and dressed myself. I put my dad's pants on, his plaid shirt, my sandals and fixed my hair into two braids. When Mrs. Sofia looked at me, she said: "Wait, you're not going to go to work like, right?" I said: "I am, the owner told me to wear something comfortable, because the work is very heavy." She replied: "I'll lend you some of my clothes, because it's your first day and it's good to make a good impression." I replied: "But he already saw me and told me to wear comfortable clothes and your clothes will be too big for me.

Don't worry, I feel good like this." She said: "For the record, I don't think it is right for you to show up like that on your first day of work." But I was used to dressing like that and I thought I looked fine. Also, at the ranch, I all my clothes was ripped and had been patched up and these were my dad's new clothes.

Well, we left earlier and took the bus with her children, so she could show me how to get there. Then, she was going to take a taxi back home. Along the way, she explained to me that I needed to pay attention to the shops on every corner, where the bus turned and when we got off the bus, I needed to remember how many right and left turns we made. She told me that I should always try to have the store's address and her address written on a piece of paper. This way, if I ever got lost, I would just take a taxi there. I felt good with all her instructions, besides, the bus took the same street on its way back. We worked from 9 AM to 2 PM, they gave us two hours so we could eat and then we worked from 4 to 8 PM. I told Mrs.

Sofia that it would be better for me if I brought something I could eat over there, because I didn't want to get lost since I only had a limited amount of time, I would go back home until nighttime. She said it was fine, that it would be better to get a taxi on my way back, so she wouldn't be so worried about me. I agreed with her.

When I arrived at the store, Mr. Raul was there, and he introduced me to his secretary. She told me that she was in charge of paying us. While I was on trial, they were going to pay me in cash. When I started working formally, they were going to pay me by check, but the company needed to have me on trial for a few more months before giving me health insurance. He told me that the insurance doctor was also his family doctor and he would take care of me in the meantime. He also introduced me to the other workers. The driver who supplied the tents was Ramón; the boy in the warehouse was named Adrian, and two girls who were manager in charge of the store.

He said that they were going to train me, because he was going to be out of town for six weeks. He was a sales agent for his brother's factory and he would travel a lot. He told me not to worry, he was leaving me in very good hands. The two girls had the same name, Antonia. One was tall and burly and the one was short and thin.

They would call one of them big Antonia and the other one was little Antonia. As soon as the owner said goodbye and left the store, everyone went to their work areas. Then, those girls started laughing out loud. I just looked at them, because I didn't know what they were laughing at. When they stopped laughing, one of the girls said: "The boss has got to be crazy if he wants to work a miracle with you. Well, he should take you to his mother's house to work as a housekeeping, because even the servants dress better than you." The big girl told me: "We're here because we shed blood and tears studying to get a university degree.

Some nobody like you, who was pulled out of the middle of nowhere, will never be on our level. Not even in your wildest dreams." The smaller girl said: "That man's head is not right if he thinks we're going to do that."Big Antoniasaid: "Well, the only thing you might be good at is this."She went and pulled out a bucket of water and a towelso I could clean and said: "You're going to clean the entire store floor, on your knees."

I said:"But there's a mop there." She replied: "The mop is for civilized people, so you're going to clean it with that. But if you don't like it, you know where the door is. You can go whenever you want, we'll just tell the owner that you didn't like the job." I said: "That's fine." That's when I understood that Mrs. Sofia was right; I didn't look good in those clothes. At around noon, I went over and said: "I'm done." The big girl answered: "Well, go and do it all over again." I went back and started doing it again and they just laughed. I spent all day there until we left at night.

Adrian, the warehouse manager, was around twenty-five to thirty years old. He had a motorcycle and he also had a lot of tattoos and wore leather jackets. He didn't speak with me, but I was afraid of him just by look at him. That boy worked a lot. The main warehouse was behind the store on the second floor. He loaded, unloadedand supplied all the merchandise for the stores.

That night, when I got home, Mrs. Sofia asked me: "How was your first day?" I said: "It's very hard, I don't think I can take it." I told her everything. She told me: "Look darling, those girls simply want you to leave before the boss returns. But you must endure that until he comes back and then you can tell him everything they did to you." I replied: "But I don't know what they're going to tell him and who he'll believe." She replied:"You have to take that risk, but you have to wait for him. Also, they're paying you very well. Savethat money so you can give it to your mom when she comes back and so she'll let you stay longer, so you can keep looking for another job."

I said: "Well, you're right about that. I'm going to put up with them just for these six weeks, because honestly, I don't know how the owner will react or who he'll believe." When they gave me my first paycheck, I told Mrs. Sofia that I was going to give her some money. She said I still wasn't sure if they were going to give me the job, so I should save it for my mom.

When they officially gave me the job, then she would take my money for staying at her house. I didn't want to spend money on clothes either, I just went and bought three pairs of sandals because I saw that mine were ugly. I cleaned the floors on my knees for two weeks, until, on one occasion, the secretary came down, went to the store for something and saw what I was doing me. She asked me why I was doing that. One of the girls told her that I didn't know how to use the mop. She told them that they were supposed to teach me.

So, she took the mop and told me how to use it and said that she didn't want to see me doing that on the floor again. I thanked God, because he used the secretary to save me from having to do that. One day, the smaller girl came in with a plastic bag, she threw it on a table and said: "I brought you some of my little sister's clothes, because I really don't know what you spend your money on but I'm tired of seeing you wearingthe same old rags every day.

And for the record, I'm only do that because you're making the rest of us look bad." The big girl started laughing and said: "Hey, you even have your own way of helping the poor." There were two pants and two blouses in the bad. I said: "Thank you." She replied: "Go and put them on right now." I put them onand they fit me. There was a factory in the back of that same building. There was some kind of patio in front of the factory. On the other side, there were stairs so you couldget to the main offices that were on the second floor. I asked the secretary if I could clean that place as well; it looked abandoned.

I spent all day locked in the store, even after I had finished cleaning everything. She gave me permission to clean it. I cleaned the entire place with water from a hose; the walls and the entire floor. I washed the white chairs with soap and some large plastic plants that were also very dirty. I arranged all the chairs and plants in one corner.

There was a table with a beach-like umbrella; I washed it as well, I opened it and arranged like a reception area. Then, when I had finished, I went to back to cleaning the store because I didn't want the managers to think I wasn't doing anything. Later that day, the secretary went looking for me because Mr. Raul's father had arrived and was surprised that everything looked so nice. He asked her who cleaned that place and he wanted to meet me. She took me to the main offices. The man told me that he wanted to meet me because he was surprised that someone had fixed that place without having been asked do so, because nobody ever does anything on their own.

He said he congratulated me because that was his house before it turned into the factory and his wife also kept it very clean. I told him that I was glad he liked it and asked him for permission to stay there during my two-hourlunch break, because I didn't like eating at home because it was too far away.

I would always sit on the floor of one of the store's aisles until the other girls got back from lunch. He said that of course I could stay there, with the condition that I kept that place clean. After that, I spent my lunch break there with some girls from the factory who also stayed there instead of going home to eat.When Mr. Raul returned six weeks later, I started shaking as soon as I saw him. He looked very happy and told the girls that he wanted to test me, to see what I had learned.But I didn't even know my way around the store, I was always in the warehouse. The big girl started saying that she was very sorry to tell him, but he had made big mistake because I wasn't good at anything.

She said I was afraid of people and, even though they tried, they couldn't get me out of the warehouse. The little girl assured him that everything she said was true, that I acted like a caveman and that I didn't even want to see people. The owner got very upset and I was able to tell that he had believed them.

I didn't know what to say, it was the two of them against me. He said: "Well time to find out for ourselves. She's going to take care of the next customer that walks through the door." He looked at me and said: "Alright girl, it's time to show me what you learned."

I was shaking, because they hadn't taught me anything. When the next customer came in, they wanted size 5 boy pants. I didn't know where the pants were, let alone the different sizes. I grabbed pants from wherever I could find them, so they could look for the size they wanted. Finally, they selected two of them.

I had to make a receipt and give it to the cashier, so she could charge them. Well, I just scribbled some lines and gave it to the cashier, hoping she would save me. But she looked at the receipt, laughed and gave it to the boss and said: "I don't understand. Do you?" When he looked at the receipt, he got very upset and asked her to make the receipt.

Then he told the other girl to close the store. When the customers left, he sat me down on a stool and started telling me that he was wrong about me. He said he thought I could learn and grow, but that wasn't the case and my time was up. From that moment on, I was fired. He said that this was a business and if someone isn't being productive, they're useless.The girls laughed and told him that they had noticed that from the beginning, but they didn't want to argue with him. I started crying, because I felt helpless because I couldn't defend myself. Suddenly, someone knocked on the door and he told them not to open the door because he wasn't finished with me yet.

He said that he really was sorry, for me and my family, but he couldn't pay me for having a pretty face, even if I was Miss Universe; the only way to get paid was by working. Suddenly, the door opened, and it was Mrs. Silvia, his wife (I didn't know her yet).

She asked them what had happened: "Why did you close the store?" He told her that she had arrived just in time, so that she would see what happened to the girl she recommended. He showed her the receipt and said: "This is what she learned during the trial we gave her." I was crouching as I cried. She said: "That also says a lot about how they trained her." He replied: "What greater proof do you want? They did everything they could and these are the results."Mrs. Silvia replied: "Well, there are still two weeks before the deadline we gave her. I'm going to take her to the other store and I'm going to train her myself.

I want to personally see if she actually doesn't work." He got upset and said: "This is over, I'm not going to spendanother penny on this girl."The lady told him not to worry, she would pay me out of her own pocket. He got even more upset and told her not to oppose him in front of his employees. She replied: "Please, don't take it that way, I just want to make sure."

Then she said: "Girl, grab your things, we're going to the other store right now." I ran to get my bag and walked out the other door. She was in charge of the store at the shopping mall with two other girls. As we were on our way there, she asked me: "What happened?" I was able to tell her everything. She asked me why I didn't call her.

I did not know her and didn't have her phone number. Actually, I didn't even know how to use a telephone. She told me: "Well, now we have a very big challenge during these next two weeks; we have to pass the test." The next day, she brought me a pile of new notebooks and books that belonged to her first-grade brothers.

She asked me to fill out entire notebooks with circles, lines, and figure eights. I would tell her: "Show me the store." She said: "Forget the store, first thing's first, you have to learn how to read and write." We were there from 8 AM until 8 PM. We didn't go out to eat; we ate there.

On the third day, my hand was very swollen from writing so much. She said that I could read the booksaloud forher little brothers while I waited for the swelling to go down. Then she had me sing all the multiplication tables until I started losing my voice. As I waited to get my voice back, I kept filing outthe little notebooks with lines and circles. When I memorized the tables, she started teaching me how to multiply, add and subtract. Three days before two weeks were over, they started teaching me how the clothes if the store was organized by sizes, styles and colors. She let me take care of all the customers and the other girls cleaned and put everything back in its place.

She asked me not to let her down, because her husband hadn't spoken to her since that argument. She said that the key when it came to sales was that when a customer was looking to buy their children pants, as they looked at them, we would bring them shirts that would match with those pants. Then, we would offer them some socks and underwear.

That always worked, customers always took something else that we had showed them. When the day of the other test arrived, it was a Monday morning, Mr. Raul walked in and didn't speak or say hello to anyone. Mrs. Silvia told the other girls that they could take a one-hour break, because this was a test and I had to do it alone.

When they left, everything was very quiet for a while, until a couple came in looking clothes for their business' inventory. They asked if we sold wholesale.(During my training, I didn't help any wholesale customers, but the lady had already taught me how to do it) They wanted dozens of everything I was showing them.

The receipt was made up only of dozens of clothes. Mrs. Silvia suggested that she would pack the merchandise while I prepared the receipt and gave it to Mr. Raul.He was sitting next to the cash register, so he could check my receipt. When I gave him the copy of the receipt, he checked it on the calculator and started laughing.

He told his wife: "What did you do with this girl? What saint pray to? Look at her beautiful handwriting. And she added it all up without even using a calculator, she didn't erase and everything's correct." He said: "I can't believe it! Well, congratulations girl, the job is yours. But don't forget what you promised me, you will be go and finish school." I was very happy, the lady and the co-workers and the other girls who recommended me, we were all very happy. They couldn't believe it, we had passed the test in just two weeks. That was truly the Lord's miracle.

I hadn't helped awholesale customer before, but I think the Lord wanted it that way, so that the owner would realize that it was something supernatural. I give all the glory and honor to my God, because only He can do such things. During the first six weeks at the other store, I would cry every night, because I was sure they were going to fire me.

I didn't know how to pray, but I believed the Lord could hear me crying every day. He sent Mrs. Silvia just in time, so she could rescue me. May his glory endure forever. The lady told her husband that she wanted to keep training me, so he would letme stay with her a while longer.

The next day, when I got to work, Mrs. Silvia brought me several bags of clothes from when she was single. Everything was very pretty and had there were even shoes. She cut my hair and told me not to braid it me again, to just use pins on the sides.

The other girls fixed my eyebrows and my nails, they put makeup on me and transformed me. When I arrived at Mrs. Sofia's house, she was also surprised. She said that this was how I should have gone to work my first day of work. Two months later, my mother returned to see what had happened to me. She was very surprised with my transformation and with all the money I had saved for them.

I'd save everything from the first two months when I was on trial test and the half of my new salary from last three weeks. Since the owner had given me a lot of clothes, I didn't buy anything, I was saving half of my salary for them. I used the other half of my salary to pay the rent and the buses I took every day, as well as my personal things. That's when I started paying the lady I was staying with for the food and rent. Mr. Raul advised me that the first thing I had to learn was how to take care of myself, but to do that I had to be responsible for all my expenses. He called one of the houses that was advertised in the newspapers and asked them how much they charged for renting that place.

He told me: "That's the right thing to do and that's how much you're going to pay wherever you might have an opportunity." Mrs. Sofia didn't want to take the money, she said it was too much. I told her that Mr. Raul told me it was enough, and I had to pay her.

She agreed, if I wanted to take his advice. Later, when I passed the test and they gave me the job, Mrs. Silvia enrolled me in an adult school that was close to the house I was living at, so that I could finish elementary school. I went to school from 6 PM to 8 PM. The lady told me that they were going to give me permission to leave at six in the afternoon. I arrived there almost at 7, but I did all my homework and I was on the same level as the other students and I passed all the exams. The teacher said that as long as I passed the exams, there wasn't any problem I arrived a little late. I finished elementary school in six months. I tried to enroll in a high school, but there were no flexible schedules.

On the other hand, Mr. Raul also started enrolling me in paid training courses for business administration, human relations and personnel training. He paid all the expenses and never deducted anything from my salary. In addition to that, all the store owners at the mall met and hired lecturers each year for leadership training.

They all sent their managers to that training. My employer would make them take turns and he would send someone different each year. But then he arranged a meeting and told them that right now, I was the one who needed it most. He told them not to feel bad, they already knew what it was about.

Everyone said it was fine. That's when I started going to those training sessions. From 9 AM until 5 PM, lunch at 12 PM and then a meal at the end.He told me to write down everything I didn't understand and then he would explain it to me. I thought of him as an older brother, always trying to help become a better person.

I wrote down everything I could, as well as the good comments other people made. These training sessions were very good. They taught us how to be leaders instead of dictators. They said that you can get much more out of a group of happy people than a group of angry people. If you treat your workers well, you will earn their respect and they will like working.

If you treat them bad, they'll hate you. If they hate you, they'll do everything to affect you, regardless of the company's interests. They said that there's a line between companies and the workers. A good leader must findbalance between the company's interests and the workers' interests.

You must care for company's interests, but you also need to consider the workers' wellbeing. If you start leaning toward one side, the employees will notice, and they won't respect you anymore. If you lean toward the other side, you'll get fired. They said that the most prosperous companies are those that have leaders instead of dictators.

I felt very good about being able to learn how to read and write. I felt as if a new world had opened before my eyes. When I took the bus that went through the center of the city, I read all the ads and knew where everything was, without having to ask anyone. I wanted to make the most of all the opportunities I was being given.

I spent my time doing my homework and reading all the books they gave us. I did that so much that, to this day, reading and writing are my favorite hobbies. The next time my mother visited, I asked her to convince my older sister to come and work in the city, because they paid us more here and she would be closer to the family.

She said she would tell her when she went to visit them. I asked a lady who had two stores at the mall and a factory if she could give my older sister a job. She replied: "If anyone works just as hard as you, bring them to me and I'll help them get a job here." Later, when my mother returned, I told her that my sister already had a job.

I was at Mrs. Sofia's house for over a year. She always treated me very well, but then she started a business and left early in the morning with her children and came back home until late at night. She told me that I could stay there, but she wouldn't have time to cook anymore, so she told me to use the money I usually gave her so I could get something to eat.

I didn't have enough to pay for breakfast, lunch and dinner at a restaurant using only what I paid her, and I didn't want to spend the money I was saving for my parents, so I decided to look for another place I could rent. I asked some of my colleagues if they knew of a place I could rent.

They said yes, that I could live with them; there were five of them and they rented a three-bedroom apartment and they didn't have a problemwith me staying with them. Every weekend, they would a party until dawn and nobody would tell them what to do.

When they lived with families, there were always a lot of problems, because if it's a young couple, the wife always gets jealous with her husband. If it's a whole family, they usually have a lot of children and they always misbehave, they don't respect your personal belongings. So, to avoid all that, several of them rented an apartment together and it was much easier for them.

I told them that it sounded great, but I made my father a promise before I left the ranch and if I went and lived with them, it would be very difficult to keepthat promise. They asked me what promise I made. I told them that, when I was about to come to the city, all my little brothers started telling me what they wanted me to buy themonce I got paid.

When I asked my dad what he wanted, he saidthat what he wanted was very hard to get. I assured him that he could ask me for anything he wanted, I would commit myself and save as much as I needed to, so I could afford it. (I thought he was going to ask for a new rifle or a shotgun, because he was a very good hunter.)

He bowed his head, stood silent for a moment and then said: "Darling, the only thing I want is for you to behave, because most girls who go to the city come back pregnant or with a child and I don't want that for you. I want you to get married, so that you will be happy for the restof your life."

That moved me a lot and I told him that I was going to promise him that, if I ever got married, he would walk me down the aisle dressed in white. Not just because of the dress, but because I would arrive at my wedding with great honor. He said that would be the greatest gift I could ever give him. I told the girls: "If I go and live with you,some drunk could rape me since you like to party so much, and I wouldn't not be able to keep that promise." They all laughed and one of them said: "Listen to the nonsense that comes out of your mouth. At this point, nobody cares about virginity. You would rather suffer and bemistreatedby families than lose your virginity."

They were all laughing uncontrollably. The next day, Mr. Raul was very serious when her arrived and told me that he wanted to speak with me, that we should go to his car. I got scared and I thought someone said something bad about me. When we arrived, he told me that his wife had overheard the conversation I had with my co-workers and that it touched her.

She asked him to give me the opportunity of staying at their house until I found somewhere else to stay. He told me: "I really want to congratulate you, because what you promised your father are values that demonstrate the kind of person you are." He said: "So, let's go get your things right now, my wife has already prepared a place for you to stay at our house." I couldn't believe it! I lived with them for about a year. He advised me that whenever I went and rented a house, I should always think of it as a temporary stay, because nobody fits in with family that's not their own.

Each family is like a different world; they all live by their own rules and convictions to educate their children. And that's true, people simply get tired of having another person in their house and the time comes when they want to have their own privacy. He said: "When you realize that things aren't going well anymore, start looking for another place, before you get kicked out."

And so, I did that. One day, a lady named Catalina went shopping at our store. She asked me how I was doing; I told her I was fine, I was just looking for a place to rent and I asked her to let me know if she knew about a place that was for rent. She said that she had a room available that I could rent. I was very excited, and I decided to move inwith her, because I didn't want Mrs. Silvia and her husband to get tired of me.Mrs. Silvia told me that it was going to be hard for her baby, because they had already gotten used to me.

I also felt bad, but another baby was on the way and they were going to need the other bedroom and I wanted to leave before they kicked me out. I told her that whenever they needed me for anything, they could count on me, because I stayed with the baby when they had to do things on the weekends. She said that they would need me on the weekends. I told her that was fine.

Mrs. Silvia taught me everything about the business. The textures of fabrics, styles and colors, how to select the combinations to decorate and make changes to the sideboards, I loved doing that. In addition to that, I learned how to balance the cash register at the end of the day, create a weekly report, how to maintain and organize the warehouse by sizes, styles and colors.

We had to immediately stock everything that was being sold so that the merchandise was always available for the customers. They also had a bus that was conditioned to be a store and they drove it to markets or flea markets.

They would sell a lot there, but none of the cashiers wanted to work in those places because there were a lot of people and we had to use the public toilets in the market. I told them that I wanted to go because that's how I practiced working in all the areas. When I learned how everything related to the stores worked, they made me a cashier and increased my salary. A year later, Mr. Raul told me it was time to make some changes.

Each year, hewould move all the workers to different stores, so that they would have a better development and coexist with the others and not get used to the same place. He told me it was time to go back to the Antonias, the other girls who were supposed to teach me, but did not.

I asked him, I begged him, I pleaded that I didn't want to go back with them. Mrs. Silvia said that he was right, sooner or later, I had to face that situation. They said that now everything would be very different, they were going to feel bad about what they did. I didn't have to worry, everything was going to be fine, and I could notify them immediately if they did or said anything to me. Well, we'll continue in the next chapter. (Maybe someone is wondering if I kept my promise and I'll tell you later, because I want to continue with the book in an orderly manner.)

Chapter 6

Facing The Enemy

Proverbs 1:10-11, 15-16, 19

10 My son, if sinners entice thee, consent thou not. 11 If they say, Come with us, let us lay wait for blood, let us lurk privily for the innocent without cause.

15 My son, walk not thou in the way with them; refrain thy foot from their path:16 For their feet run to evil, and make haste to shed blood.

19 So are the ways of every one that is greedy of gain; which taketh away the life of the owners thereof.

When I returned to the store downtown one year later, the workers there had a very different attitude. They told me they wanted me to show them what I had learned. They let me do all kinds of things at the store. From cleaning to serving customers, charging them and then I had to put everything I had shown them back in its place. They would sit around, making jokes and even if started getting crowded, they wouldn't get up.

Whenever I asked them: "Can you help me please?" They answered: "Of course, boss, you're the boss now." And they always laughed at everything. I remained very serious time, because I already knew them and didn't want to give them a reason to make fun of me. Sometime later, Adrian, the boy from the warehouse, offered to drive me home on his motorcycle. I thanked him, but I was already used to riding the bus.

He said he was going to wait for me outside. I stayed a while longer to wait for him to leave, but when I left, he was still waiting outside. He said he was waiting for me, he just wanted to be my friend. I told him that I respected him as a work colleague, but after work, I was not interested in his friendship.

I asked him to please go and leave me alone. The bus arrived, I got on and he was still following me. When I got off the bus, he followed me to my house. The next day, I told Mr. Raul what he did. I asked him to please tell him to leave me alone, I was focused on my classes and had a lot of things to do.

Right now, the most important thing for me was to improve myself. He told me not to worry, he was going to take care of that, they were friends since high school and he knew his family.The following week, when we went to the market, Adrian was upset. He said he couldn't believe I had told the owner about that.

I replied: "I did it because you didn't respect what I said, and I thought that he would be the only person you'd respect. So, please, let's keep everything as it has been until now. I respect you and admire you for you work, but nothing more." He replied: "It's okay, I'll do as you say.

When we leave this place, we'll be like two strangers." From that point on, he didn't say a word to me at work again. When I brought him orders for the goods I needed, he just grabbed the receipt and didn't say a single word. A while later, the girls started being very kind to me. They told me they wanted to invite me to go out somewhere.

I said no, but I thanked them very much. Then, the small girl invited me to eat at her house. I told her I was grateful, but I couldn't go, because the lady I lived with had a curfew and I didn't want to cause any problems, so they wouldn't kick me out.Then, they invited me to the movies, they told me to tell the lady ahead of time.

I said no again and thanked them, but I had a lot of homework I had to do before I went to bed. The big one asked me: "Tell us, what do we have to do to gain your trust? Are you ever going to forgive us for mistakes?" I said: "I don't have anything against you, I just have other things to do.

I'm studying, and I have a lot homework. I need to make up for the time I wasted when I didn't go to school. She said: "Well, at least join us for an ice cream and live a little." I replied: "For me, the time we spend here together at work is more than enough. We spend all day together here, what more do you want?" She replied: "Apparently, we can't convince you, right?

But we're not the ones to give up, so we'll keep insisting until you go somewhere with us." A little while later, one day that Mr. Raul went to the store, the big one told him that he always said that all workers should share and try to get along with each other during work hours. He said that was best for everyone.

She told him that they were tired of inviting me to go somewhere and always getting rejected. They only wanted to erase the bad impression I had about them, but I would always refuse. Now, they were inviting me to get some ice cream and I didn't want to do that. They asked him for permission, so I would accompany them.

He told them that was fine and told me to go and get some ice cream with them. I said I was sorry, but I had a lot of homework and couldn't go. He insisted that I make plans to accompany them one day, that it that was very good for us. She said to set aside one day next week, it would only be for half an hour after getting offwork.

I told them I was going to think about it, to see which day I could set aside. I told Mrs. Silvia what her husband had said, it was as if he was making me go out with them. She told me not to worry, that she was going to talk to him because she didn't feel good about forcing me into something I didn't want to do.

Afterwards, she told me that her husband was right; if they had asked him for permission, it was because they had good intentions, because if they did something to me, they would have to answer to him. She said: "Decide where you're going to go with them and let us when and where you're going out with them.

Maybe they really want to make things right with you. "I told the girls I would go out with them, that we would go out on Wednesday (so it wouldn't be a weekend) and that they would tell me where the ice cream shop was. They agreed and told me not to worry, that it was an ice cream shop that was very close, just around the corner from work.

When we left work at 8 PM, they started laughing a lot. One said: "Finally we were able to enjoy your presence. You punished us for almost a year with your rejection." They continued laughing. I didn't answer them, and I was very seriousbecause I sensed something.

I tried looking to see which streets we were walking down, but every time they came to a corner they said: "Which street is it?" They acted as if they didn't remember where the place was and kept walking. We walked a lot, taking several turns, from one side toanother, and they completely confused me. I didn't know where we were.

I said: "Well, if you don't remember the place, we should just go back, because I told the lady whose house I'm staying at that I was going to arrive half an hour late." They said: "There's no way we're going back now, we're almost there." Suddenly, one of them said: "Look, there it is, on the other side of the street."

When I turned around to look at the other street, the two of them grabbed meby one of my arms and they quickly pushed me into some place.They distracted me in such a way that I didn't know where they were taking me. According to them, they were just playing the whole time and they told me we had arrived.

The place was very dark, there were tables and I knew it was a. They sat me in a corner all the way at the back and one of them sat on each side. The waitresses there knew them, greeted them and they told her: "You already know what to bring us." I told them: "This isn't an ice cream shop."

They laughed and told the waitresses: "The girl wants her ice cream." They all laughed. I looked at the door in the distance and big Antonia said: "Don't even think about it, you're not leaving this place." When the waitress came back with three beers, I took advantage of the fact that she was standing next to the biggest girl and I said to them:

"Well, you told me it was a nice cream shop and that's not true, so I'm leaving." I quickly got up and went to side the smaller Antonia was. The big one yelled: "Don't let her escape!" The smaller one grabbed me by my pants at around my knees, but I hit her hand very hard and she let me go. I ran to the door as fast as I could, but I couldn't push the door to open it, I had to pull it.

Once I opened the door, the smaller Antonia grabbed my hair with both hands and pulled me down very hard. She was a little shorter than me. I turned on my side, put my two hands together, punched her as hard as I could with my elbow and she fell to the floor.

The other girl was running toward me, but when she saw that the other girl fell, she bent over to pick her up and that's when I opened the door again and ran out. They also chased after me. I ran as fast as I could, but when I got to the intersections, I didn't know where to go and they almost caught up to me.

I was still running desperately, until I saw a busy avenue in the distance and I went there. Big Antonia was tall and burly, the other one was short and thin, but the girl ran very fast and the bigger one kept yelling at her, telling her not to let me get away, to grab me by one foot and throw me to the ground so she could grab me.

When I got to the avenue, I saw a bus that was on the opposite side of the street, so I ran across the street. The bus hit the brakes and the tires squealed and I ran inside the bus. The driver got upset and yelled: "Stupid girl, if you want to kill yourself, go kill yourself, but don't put all these people's lives at risk."

I was shaking and said: "They're chasing me," as I started crying. They stood on the other side of the street and when all the people turned to look at them, they ran away. The driver asked me: "Do you know them?" I just shook my head and said yes. The driver told me: "Sit here. Next to him, on the floor."

I sat down and he asked me where I was going. I told him I wanted to take the bus that passed through the San Marcos garden. He said he drove by that place, he would tell me when we were there. I pulled out money to pay him, but he didn't want it. When we arrived, he told me: "Here we are, but don't run anymore, walk calmly, because you're going to cause an accident, and nobody is chasing you." I thanked him. As soon as I got off the bus, I ran as fast as I could to get to the house. When Mrs. Silvia arrived, I told her everything. She told her husband that he had to call the police.

He said there weren't enough charges and the police couldn't do anything, they were only going to cause me more problems, it would be better if we acted as if nothing had happened. He told me to never trust them again or eat anything they gave me. The next day, I arrived to work as if nothing had ever happened. I smiled as I greeted everyone: "Good morning," and I started doing my job.

They were very quiet and didn't talk or laugh; it was like that for a while. About three or four months later, on a Friday when we were working in the market, Adrian, the boy from the warehouse, told me that it was his last day working there because he was moving somewhere very far, and no one was going to hear from him.

I told him that he didn't have to quit his job over little things like what had happened, our employer paid us very well and he liked him because he was a very good worker. He told me that it wasn't because of the work, he was already tired of that life and wanted to go far away, where no one knew him, so he could start over.

But before he left, he just wanted to give me some advice: he told me to go back to my parents, because the city was very dangerous. He told me that his mother always advised him to get a good woman, so he could turn his life around. He said he always thought about it, but he hadn't met anyone.

He said that when I started working there, he always looked at me like a girl, but when I came back from the other store a year later, he was impressed by how they had transformed me. He thought that I could be the woman he was looking for, but when I rejected him and told the boss what happened, he realized that he really wasn't going to be able to do anything and that made him very angry. When the girls found out, they told him that they were going to help him get revenge on me and they sold me out so that he and his friends could do whatever they wanted with me and then they would get rid of me.

He said they paid them, and everything was ready, they rented an apartment for a few days. The girls were going to take me somewhere and they were going to drug me. Then, he and his friends would take a car and pick me up. When they arrived to pick me up, the girls made up a story that I had escaped.

He said that they thought the boss was going to do something to them, but the next day, everyone showed up as if nothing had ever happened. So they didn't believe them and they made them return the money. He said that the ladies at the bar also said it was true, but they didn't believe them and thought that the other girls had paid them. He asked me if that was true. I replied: "Yes, it's true, but since there was no evidence, Mr. Raul said that the police couldn't do anything. He said it was better to act as if nothing had happened to avoid more problems." He replied: "Well, apparently you have an angel that takes care of you." He said: "I just wanted to mention this so that you realize what those women are capable of."

You should just return to your town, because they won't leave you alone. They can't forgive because, no matter how hard they tried to stop you, you were able to turn your life around without having studied and now you earn just as much as the others. For your own sake, go back to your family."

I replied: "Well, I appreciate your advice and since we're speaking truthfully, can I say something?" He replied: "Sure." I said: "If you say you really want to start a new life, first you need to change the way you dress, cover or remove those tattoos. Because the first time I saw you, I was afraid just by looking at you, and you never offended me or addressed me at all.

First, change your appearance and you'll see how everything will be easier for you." He laughed and said he thought he looked good. I replied: "I thought the same thing about myself, I thought I looked fine with my clothes from the ranch, but everyone laughed at me and now that I've made the changes, they all look at me differently.

The same thing will happen to you." He laughed again and said he was going to try to do that. He asked me not to tell anyone anything, because he didn't want to be found. He asked me to forgive him for the things he made me go through and he wished me the best. I told him not to worry, it was all in the past and I thanked him for his advice.

The next day, he didn't come back. Some people asked and others said that maybe he had gone drinking and slept in. On Monday, when he didn't show up for work, everyone started to worry. The owner went and looked for him at his house and his mother didn't know anything about him, she was crying a lot. I felt very bad, but I couldn't say anything. At that time, Mr. Raul and his wife had bought a house and, coincidentally (well, that's what you think, but the Lord has a plan and a purpose for everything), he said that one day he went out to clean his patio and realized that one of his neighbors was big Antonia's father.

They spoke for a while and they seemed liked very good people; he was retired and had his own house. (Their daughter had said she lived at another address, but nobody knew where she lived.) They became friends with her parents and they told me not to worry anymore, at least now they knew them and where she lived.

Shortly after, when the year was over, they made changes again and big Antonia and I got transferred to the store at the shopping mall, along with two other girls who worked during that season. When the winter season passed, the owner told us to put all the winter merchandise at half price.

One Friday, some customers came and asked me if we had enough assortment of coats, because they wanted to buy wholesale. I told them we did. Antonia was quick and removed the advertisements for the sale and asked me if they had already asked for the price. I told her they hadn't.

She said to charge them the normal price. The customers never asked about the prices, they just checked the price on the tags and bought everything we had in stock. She made the receipt and charged them, but she didn't register it in the cash register. When they left, she made another receipt with the discounted price and registered it in the cash register.

Then she started counting the money and separated it into several piles and said: "Here, this is your share." I replied: "No, thank you, I don't want anything." She said: "This isn't stealing, it's just being smart and knowing how to do business. Nobody stole anything; the client took his merchandise and we put their money there." I replied:

"Well, if you see it that way, that's fine, but I'm not going to be a part of that, nor am I going to go around and tell on you. Everyone is responsible for their own actions." She got a bit upset and said: "It's not about whether you're going to be a part of this or not, you saw what we did and you're a part of it."

I said: "Don't wrap me up in all of this; everyone is responsible for their decisions and I decided not to be a part of it." She was very upset and said: "Don't you understand? I'm not asking you for your opinion, this is a business, several are people involved and now you're a part of it as well."

I replied: "I didn't do anything, you did it and you'retrying to get me mixed up with your things. If that sounds good to you and doesn't affect anyone else, then keep doing it, but I'm not going to be a part of that." That's when she got angry and started cursing. She said that I was already a part of that, they had already planned everything.She said that the gentleman from the bank who visited them often was also involved. He had their accounts at the bank and would collect their money every other day. They did it that way so no one would catch them with money on them and he also had his share. Every one of them had to give him a commission. She said: "This is a gold mine.

If you know how to work smart, you'll stop being poor. In other words, so you can understand me better, this is a gang and you already belong to it. But if you don't want to be a part of it, as you already know, we're going to have to cut your head off. We're not going to risk you blowing our cover. But if you work for us, you won't regret it and you'll be able to help your family out."

I told her: "You think that I'm capable of betraying the ones who helped me?" She replied: "Well, you decide, you only have two options: either you're in or you won't see your family again. We're not going to lose our business because of your stupidity."She went and put the money in my bag. I didn't know what to do. I thought about everything the boy from the warehouse had told me before leaving, that I should return to my family. I thought it would be for the best. That afternoon, I called the store owner and told her that they told me that my father was sick, and I wanted to go see him on Sunday.

I asked if they could give me some days off. She replied: "Sure, take the entire week if you like or take both of your vacation weeks if you want to. I'll let my husband know." I thanked her. That night, I got home and started crying as I packed all my things, so I didn't have to come back. I thought long and hard about it, but I had no other way out.

I couldn't be an accomplice and betray the trust of those who helped me out so much. I couldn't sleep as I thought and cried, planning what I was going to do. I thought about leaving and then, once I was there, sending them a letter to thank them for everything they did for me, explaining everything that had happened and why I couldn't go back. On Saturday morning, when I took the bus to work, I ran into Mr. Raul on the bus, he never did that. When Adrian left, the one from the warehouse, he would take the bus to the market and the other man, Mr. Ramon, would take his car and drive on his way back.

It just so happened that that day, Mr. Ramon couldn't go to work and he sent a boy to cover for him, but the boy didn't know how to drive, so he had to take the bus back.Since hesaw that I was crying, he told me that he was very sorry about my dad, that his wife had already told him everything.

He said I could take as much time as I needed, my job would always be there waiting for me. I felt even worseand I started crying. He said: "What happened to your dad?" Suddenly, I didn't know what to say and I said: "I don't know, they just told me he was very sick." It seemed a bit strange to him, because there were no telephones at the ranch, we wouldsend each other letters and we had to go to the villageif we wanted to make a call. In addition to that, the house I was living at didn't have a telephone either, they could only call me when I was at the store. On the other hand, he had gone hunting with my dad on several occasions and he knew the area very well, that's why it was very difficult to lie to him. He said: "Who went to the village to make the call?"

I told him one of my sisters did. He answered: "She couldn't tell you what your dad had?" I looked down, shaking my head and said no. He answered: "You know, I feel like you're lying to me. You better tell me the truth. What happened? Did you have a problem with the girls again?" I replied: "No, it's not that. I just want to go see my dad."

He said: "Let's see, look me in the eyes." But I couldn't look him in the eyes, I was looking down. He said: "It's better if you tell me the truth. What happened?" I replied: "Okay, I'm going to tell you, but only under one condition." He said: "What's your condition?" I said: "You won't do anything until I'm at the ranch with my family."

He replied: "I give you my word, you can leave peacefully on Sunday and I'll take care of everything." I told him everything. He assured me that I didn't have to worry, I could go peacefully and take as long as I needed, but he asked me to come back, because they needed me.

We agreed on that. I felt like I had gotten rid of a great burden and I was calmer. However, at noon, Mrs. Silvia arrived with the smaller Antonia, from the store downtown. She left her there and took the bigger Antonia. My heart was pounding. Antonia asked me: "What happened? Why did they do this?

They went for me and brought me here without any explanation and now they took her. I don't like this at all, something very serious must have happened." That evening, at around 7 PM, Mrs. Silvia came to close the store and said that she was going to take me to my house. On our way home, she told me not to worry; I didn't have to go to the ranch anymore, the problem had been solved. I told her that her husband promised that he wouldn't do anything until I went to the ranch. She said they went and spoke with her dad and her brother. The owner of the factory and her family advised them that something had to be done immediately.

They called the lawyers who helped them with issues at the factory, so they could advise them on what they could do and protect me at the same time. They recommended that they call the police, so they would go to the offices at the factory and take Antonia there as well. The lawyers prepared everything and made her sign her resignation, with the charges the police gave her.

They were going to let her go, as long as she didn't come near me or the store again and they made her sign a restraining order. I got even more scared and said: "But you already know her, she's not going to respect that."

She said: "Please, do not be like that. We have to show these people that the laws are made to protect us, not to let them do whatever they want. Believe me, everything is fine, but you can't leave now until we've train some other girls. Once everything has passed, you can go on vacation." I couldn't sleep because I was so. That Sunday, I had the day off and I didn't leave the house at all.

On Monday morning, I woke up very early and left two hours earlier, because I thought Antonia was going to be waiting for me on the way to work. When I got to work, I was very surprised that the other Antonia had already opened the store. I said: "You arrived very early." She answered: "Did you think you were the only one who woke up early?"

As soon as I walked in, she locked the door and said: "They're looking for you over there." I looked around and there was nobody there. She said: "Go inside the bathroom." I replied: "I don't want to go inside the bathroom." Then, the bigger Antonia came out of the bathroom, dressed like a rocker.She was all dressed in black and wearing black boots that men use for work. She wore a black blouse, black gloves, with a leather vest and a black band tied around her head. In addition to that, she had a club in her hand. I froze when I saw her. She told me: "Did you really think you were going to get away with that? No, you must pay for everything you did to me.

Do you know what they did to me? I had worked for this company for over 10 years. I met their entire family, I gained their trust and I built a reputation, and now, because of you, they took me to the factory and made me sign my resignation for being a thief in front of everyone who knows me.

Did you really believe that I was going to be very calm as if nothing had happened?" I was shaking, unable to say anything. She said: "Well no, you're going to pay dearly for everything you did to me." She grabbed me by my hair and put me in the bathroom.

She told me: "For starters, you're going to get down on your knees and ask me to forgive you and then you'll kiss my feet." With one hand, she pulled me down by my hair and she used her other hand to beat me with the club. I fell to my knees and she kept hitting me in the back very hard, screaming at me to kiss her feet, so I kissed them. She laughed hysterically and told the other girl to come and see was doing to me.

Both laughed a lot. As I was there on my knees, I had a thought in my mind that came to me like a movie of when I was a little girl, how whenever I played with my brothers in the field, we ended up fighting and I wasn't afraid of any of them. I felt very hot and full of anger.

I got up and said: "You only have yourself to blame for what happened to you, because you didn't know how to value the trust, they gave you, so don't blame me for your bad decisions." She started laughing and told the other girl: "Would you look at that, this one has some guts." She said: "Well, because of what you just did, I'll give you another chance. Because you know very well that, right now, I can do whatever I want with you. But since I see you have some guts, from now on, you'll work for me. I lost my job because of you and now you're going to give me whatever I want. You can't imagine the power that I have, you will live as long as I want you to live. All I have to do is snap my fingers and someone will cut your head off."

She would ask the other girl if what she was saying was true. The other girl said that I had no idea who I was messing with, that it would be wise of me to obey everything she said if I wanted to see my parents again.I replied: "Well, you can do whatever you want, but I'm not going to work for you.

I would rather go back to my house, with my family, before I betray those who helped me." She said: "Who said you were going to leave the city? From now on, you belong to me and you will do whatever I say." She told the other Antonia: "I have to go now but keep an eye on her. Teach her that she has to submit to me, otherwise, she already knows what'll do to her." When she left, I sat on the stairs and started crying. The other started telling me that I didn't know what I had done and questioning why I dared challenging her. Others had lost their heads for much less. She told me that there she hung out with a lot of very powerful people that obeyed her blindly, I was going to live until she wanted me to.

A little later, Mrs. Silvia came in and said: "What happened to you? Don't tell me that the other girl threatened you?" I shook my head and said no. She asked Antonia what had happened. She said that she didn't know anything. Mrs. Silvia grabbed me by my arms and shook me as she desperately begged me to react and tell her everything that had happened. She asked: "Did she threaten you?"

I said: "She was here." She replied: "That can't be possible, that woman has to see that the police don't play around," and ran away. The other Antonia didn't say anything, she was also scared and didn't go back to work. I didn't go anywhere to eat; I stayed there all day. In the afternoon, Mrs. Silvia came back and said that now everything had been taken care of. They went to the lawyers and they prepared other papers and told them to take the police and everything she signed to their parents' house and explain everything that had happened to them.

In addition to that, they also had them sign a letter saying that if anything happened to me, accidentally or purposely, they would be responsible for the medical expenses, hospital and compensating my family in case of death, and their daughter would be imprisoned for the rest of her life. Mrs. Silvia said that it was very hard.

Her parents didn't know anything about what their daughter had been doing and they cried a lot. They said they were going to send her to another city, with their son who was a policeman, and they were going to take care of her. They told me not to worry, they were going to take care of their daughter. She showed me the copies of all the papers they signed. The lawyers and the policemen also had copies of those papers. The man who worked at the bank was also apprehended, because the bank filed charges against him as well. I told her that I wanted to go on my vacation because I felt very bad. She agreed, but she asked me to give them a week until they hired some other girls.

She said the secretary and her husband were going to help me during those days, so they would pick me up in the morning and take me home at night. I told them that was fine. Mr. Raul told me to take all the time I needed, but they wanted me to come back. I didn't say anything, because I wasn't planning on coming back.

Chapter 7

The Recovery Phase

Psalm 37: 27-28, 34.

Depart fromevil and do good; and dwell forevermore. For the Lord loves justice and does not forsake His faithful ones.

Wait on the Lord, and keep His way, and He shall exalt you to inherit the land; when the wicked are cut off, you shall see it.

When I went on vacation, I was determined to not go back. I kept the best of my clothes in two cardboard boxes and threw away the rest. I just left a few of my oldest blouses, so they lady whose house I was staying at wouldn't say anything. That way, in case the owner asked her, she would say she didn't know anything.

Then, I would send them a letter to let them know that my father didn't let me go back. (I had everything planned out, but the Lord had other plans) On Monday, I sent my parents a telegram that this was arriving in three days. Since everyone in the village knows each other, they would give it to some family member and they would ask someone we knew to deliver it to the ranch, so that they would wait for me at the village next Sunday.

When I arrived, the first news my dad gave me shook my heart. He told me that my older sister had come back from Laredo, Texas, to go to work with me in the city. The first thing I thought was that I made her quit her job and now, how am I going to tell her that I'm not going back? I felt very bad, but I didn't mention anything to my dad. Something elsemy dad did that day, which he'd never done before, was that whenever people greeted him and asked him what he was doing, he would happily say: "I came to pick up my daughter who's on vacation.

She works in the city and earns a lot of money, more than my daughter in the United States, and she is going to take her back to the city to, so she can also work with her." My heart was aching, and I said: "Dad, please don't say that. We're going to walk through the hills for three hours, they could chase us to mug us and I didn't bring money." He said: "No, the people from the ranch don't do that."

Even though we were walking through the mountains on our way home, he kept saying the same thing to everyone we met, and they asked him where he came from. That was when I realized that he was very proud of me. How was I going to tell him that I wasn't going back? All those people he talked to were going to laugh at him. I went ahead, riding my donkey, crying, and he was very happy and whistling on another donkey behind me. When we finally got home, the only one I told was my older sister. We went for a walk in the mountains and I said: "And now the hardest thing is, how am I going to tell dad?

If I tell him, he's not going to let me go back and he told all those people that I was on vacation, now they're all going to laugh at him. I can't do that. I should just go back and leave it in God's hands." She replied: "Don't worry, God knows why he lets things happen. I'm also going to be with you now. Maybe the parents will control their daughter.

We're going to pray and ask God to give her a good man she can marry, so she'll be happy and won't want to hurt anyone else. When people are happy, they don't want to do anything that'll hurt others." I said: "Why don't we pray that she dies? There's a saying that says: Dead dogs don't bite." She said: "No, we shouldn't wish that for anyone;anything that you wish unto others will also happen to you." I felt a little calmer with my sister and we went back two weeks later. On the Sunday that I came back, I called Mrs. Silvia to let her know that I had returned.

She said she would be waiting for me at the shopping mall location the next day. When I arrived on Monday, the lady introduced me to the new girls as the person in charge and gave me the keys to the store. She told me that they decided to leave the new girls with me so I could train them and so they would get used to me and make a good team.

I told her that was fine. A few days later, I asked Mrs. Silvia if she'd let me make some changes. She said if the store would benefit from those changes, I could make as many changes as I wanted. I mentioned that I had noticed that during the time we closed to go to eat, from 2 to 4 PM, we lost a lot of customers. Some people asked us at what time we came back and by the time we came back, they were already gone. Most of them came from villages two or three hours away to buy merchandise for their businesses. Waiting two hours was a waste of time for them; they would finish their purchases at around five or six in the afternoon and they would get back to their villages at night.

However, if they bought from two to four, they had enough time to get back home on time. I told her I was going to send a girl to lunch from 1 to 3 PM and the other one from 3 to 5 PM and I would eat there. In addition to that, we wouldn't have a fixed schedule when we closed at night, we would close once the last client we were attending had left.

Because sometimes they rushed them or kicked them out, so they could close the store. I also wanted to ask them to the girls who stayed to help me overtime, because that wasn't mandatory, it was optional. She said that it seemed like a good idea to her and that, if I wasn't going to go out to eat, then they would pay for my food and I could take money from the cash register to buy my lunch. We did that, and the store's sales increased a lot. Those girls and I made a great team. I told them that on Saturdays, or whenever they didn't want to go home to eat, we could order food; we would pay half of it from the cash register and we would split the other half between the three of us.

They could use their two hours to go see the other stores or just to rest in the warehouse. One day, they told me that girls from the other stores told them to make me give them their lunch at two o'clock, from 2 to 4 PM, because their employers realized we sold a lot during that time.

Most stores closed during that time and eventually they were going to force them to do the same thing we did. They said that they told them they didn't want to, they liked that schedule because there weren't so many people on the buses at that time of the day and they would get home a lot faster and they would have more time to do things. It was a good idea to give them that schedule. My sister also started working at a store right there at the mall. We lived at the same place and we would always go out together. I started going to church with her and that helped me a lot to overcome everything that had happened.

One day, a man came to our store he was the owner of the store next door (the one who didn't let me work at his store) went to talk with Mrs. Silvia; they were talking for a while as we worked. As he was leaving, Mrs. Silvia said: "Have you seen the girl you didn't want? She's one of my best workers."

He replied: "I noticed and now that you mention it, I want to apologize to this girl right here, in public. To be honest, I didn't know her, I got carried away by what they told me about her." He said: "I'd like to offer you my apologies and, whenever you like, there will always be work for you at my store." I told him not to worry, everything happens for a reason and we must make the best out of everything that happens to us. On another occasion, the man returned and told me he was serious about his offer. If I decided to go to work for him, he would paytwice as much as my employers paid me and I could decide which store I wanted to work at.

He also had several stores and a factory. I thanked him for the offer and told him that they paid me very well, besides it wasn't all about the money, I was very grateful for everything they did for me. He said that he really admired me and deeply regretted not having given me a chance.

One day, a sister from Church asked me to talk to Mr. Raul to see if he would give a girl who was about to finish college a job, because she needed to work to pay for her studies. From October to December, they always hired extra people for the Christmas season and depending on how good they were, they would call them when they needed them. I told the owner that I had been told that she was a very good, responsible girl that also went to Church. He told me to tell her to apply, because the good season was coming and he needed to train personnel. A week after she started working, she asked all of us what we'd studied. One day, we arrived, and we all started working, but she was just sitting there.

Suddenly, I asked her: "Do you feel okay?" She said yes, she felt great. I said: "What's going on then? You don't want to work today?" She replied: "I don't take orders from ignorant people and if you want to be my boss, you have to go to college first." I said: "So, in the meantime, are you just going to sit there? Did they teach you the definition of the word work at school?

Because you're getting paid to do your job, not to come here and investigate if we've studied or not. If you don't feel like working today, you can go home. If you sit there, I'm going to have to file a report, that's part of my job. Now, decide if want to work or go home." She got up and started working. She would always complain about something different. The other workers told me: "Don't let her disrespect you, report her."I felt embarrassed of going to the owner, because I had recommended her and told himwonders about her. I didn't know how to tell him what was happening. I also thought about the people from Church, they were going to say that I had gotten her fired.

One day, Mr. Raul called me and asked me to close from two to four because he needed to talk to meand we would meet at the office downtown. When I arrived, he asked me if the girl I'd recommended was my friend. I said no, I only knew her parents because they went to church sometimes.

He said that I should consider her my worst enemy then, because she went and told him that I wasn't qualified for that position, because without education, all I was doing was discrediting his company. She told him that she had a friend who had just graduated from university and she'd already talked to her and she was willing to take my place. He told me that he just wanted to let me know that they were going to fire her, because she betrayed the person who had helped her out. Not just that, she did it behind my back and she was already offering someone else my job. He said that a person is unethical, someone who lacks values, who only cares about positions so they canhave control over others. They're capable of doing anything to feed their ego, completely disregarding thecompany's wellbeing, let alone the workers'wellbeing.

Young people, this is what happens in the real world; when you haven't studied, and you start working, it isn't just bullying anymore, it's hatred, envy, because money and poweris involved. You'll run into people that want to get rid of you just, so they can take your place.

I realized that a person with a college degree doesn't support a supervisor who didn't go to school. That girl gave me the most trouble. The other girls who got transferred from the other stores each yearwere somewhat aggressive at the beginning, but I told them that if they weren't willing to be flexible when it came to closing time, then they would be have to arrive on time. Because sometimes, when it was time to close, people would start to gather around, and nobody wanted to stay and help. They would tell me: "You have to do what the other stores do, close the store 15 minutes before closing time and kick the customers out at 8 PM.

I would tell them: "But we spend most of the day sitting down and they pay us for not doing anything and when the customers arrive, you want to kick them out? The ones who generate the income for the business and pay for our salaries? That doesn't seem fair to me. How about we make up for that time we spent doing nothing when customers arrive?

Now, if you can't stay for some reason, you can leave, nobody is going to force you to stay. This is about being conscious and working as a team." As soon as they got the hang of things, we made a very good team, for the most part.They swapped their lunch breaks when they had to do something, they were covered for each other when they had a doctor's appointment or school. At the other stores, they didn't cover for each other; if they had something to do, they didn't get paid and whoever did that person's work got paid overtime.So, some of them earned more and others earned less.

I told them: "Nobody has to earn less if you cover for each other on you rest days or swap your lunch breaks." They all agreed and that's what we did. On one occasion, the owner told me: "What do you do to your girls? Every time they get transferred to another store, your girls crywhen they leave, and the others are excited.

And the same thing happens every year; the ones who were happy are crying now and the others are happy." I said: "We just try to work as a team." A few years later, Mrs. Silvia told me that her neighbors had told her that Antonia had gotten married to a great man in the other city and she was expecting her first baby. I told her that was my sister's prayer, that she would be happy and stop hurting people. It was difficult to imagine that, but sometime later, some very elegant ladies arrived at the store. I was at the cash register, it was a very busy day. A lady came over and quietly asked me: "Don't you recognize me?"

I looked at her and her face was familiar, but I didn't know where I'd seen her before. She told me: "It's probably better that you don't remember me." She turned around and started laughing and that's when I recognized her laughter; it was Antonia, but she didn't look like herself. I said: "I remember your voice, but you don't look like yourself anymore."

She laughed even more and left with her friends. She was thin and looked very tall, with long hair and a dress. She never dressed like that. If I hadn't heard her voice, I would've never recognized her. One day, as I was talking with Mrs. Silvia, I told her that the other Antonia seemed like a good person, maybe the same thing that they wanted to do to me had happened to her. If she found out what they were doing, they forced her to join them. She said that she thought the same thing too.One day, a few years later, when I was about to get married, Mr. Raul arrived at the shopping mall store. We were all very busy with clients. He just walked in, left and he didn't come back.

After a while, I asked the girls if he had already left. One of the girls went out to see where he was and when she came back, she said that heat the shops downstairs, talking to a man. I went over to see, and he was with a man in a gray suit, the man was facing the other direction.When Mr. Raul came in, I said: "We thought you'd already left."

He answered: "No, I was talking with someone. Did you see who it was?" I said: "No, he was facing the opposite direction." He said: "So you didn't recognize him?" I said: "No." He told me that it was Adrian, the boy from the warehouse, the one who'd disappeared. I asked: "Why didn't you bring him? I wanted to see him." He said: "He didn't want to come because he was embarrassed of running into you. He told me that he got married to a great girl and he has two children." I was glad that they were able to turn their life around and start their own family. My sister was right, when a person's happy, they stop harming others.

When my sister moved to the city, I also told her about what Mrs. Carmen, the lady I worked with when I first arrived had done to me so she wouldn't talk to her. But my sister told me it was quite the opposite, that lady needed to learn about God and she was going to try to get her to go to church.

I was upset with my sister and I asked her not to do that, but she didn't listen to me and instead of eating and taking her days off, she would go and help her just, so she could tell her about the Lord and take her to church. A few months later, she took her to church and she gave her life to the Lord. I was also starting to go, but we didn't talk to each other. When I was sitting at the front, she would sit at the back and when she was at the front, I would sit as far back as possible.Until one day, a guest preacher was invited to our church and he gave a strong sermon about forgiving one another. He waited to take the tithes and offering until the end and said: "Nobody is going to give their offering until they've reconciled with their neighbor."

I was sitting at the front and I thought to myself: "She was the one who offended me. She has to come to me." It was almost as if the preacher knew what I was thinking and said: "You don't ask for forgiveness instead of the person who offended you, you ask for your own liberation; the benefit is for you, not for the one who offended you."

As I was going to turn around, she walked up next to me. That was when we saw each other eye to eye again and we apologized to one another. Some years later, when I was going to get married, Mrs. Carmen gave me a wedding gift, an envelope with money inside. It was a Friday and the wedding was on Saturday evening. When we got home, I opened it and it was a lot of money. My husband said: "She must have made a mistake and mixed that envelope up with the sales envelope from her store. I should pick you up early tomorrow, so we can return it to her.

That way, she can give whatever she's going to give you for our honeymoon." The next day, we went to give it back to her and she said: "No, I didn't make a mistake. That's your wedding gift." It was the equivalent of the six months of salary she hadn't paid me, twice as much as she owed me. So, she regretted what she did and paid back twice as much.

How many times have we asked for forgiveness of our sins and believed that once we had asked for forgiveness our debts were paid? It is one thing to ask for forgiveness and it's a completely different thing to pay our debts. Restoration is part of your liberation. She was completely freed by the Lord and so was I; I completely forgot any grudge and I asked the Lord to bless her, because not everyone would do what she did. With time, I was able to understand that every one of these people was part of my process. I paid a very high price for dropping out of school, that's why I wanted to share this with you and motivate you to reflect a little bit.

Don't drop out of school, because your future and your family's wellbeing depend on that. For those of you who've dropped out of school, it's never late to start. It'll cost you a bit more, because of your work and your family, but it can be done and it's worth it.

Sometimes when we feel fulfilled with a professional career or a good job, we seem to forget our beginnings. Instead of helping someone in need, we demand even more from them than we could ever give. Positions and good jobs aren't for life, they can change overnight. In life, there are lots of ups and down, things can change from one day to the next and what you did for someone, someone else will do for you or someone in your family. That's why we should try to be humble and reach out to those in need. "Obviously without committing ourselves to things that we shouldn't do."

Just remember that the child or teenager you helped in one way or another, so they could finish their studies could become the supervisor, engineer or lawyer that will on day help your children or grandchildren. I want to thank Mrs. Silvia and her husband Raul for investing their time and money in me to transform my life.

Even though they knew I wasn't good at anything, they took me in, gave me an opportunity at their business and opened their house and hearts. I will forever be grateful for what they did for me. I pray that, in our Lord Jesus' name, God the Father will extend his hand upon their family and always bless them with his presence.

Chapter 8

Keeping A Promise

Hebrews 13:4

Marriage is honorable among all and the bed undefiled: but fornicators and adulterers God will judge.

Adulterers are all those who have intimate relationships with another person while being married. Fornicators are all those who have intimate relationships without being married. When I promised my father that he was going to walk me down the aisle dressed in white, I did it, so I could see the great love he had for me and because he only wanted what was best for me. I never thought that such a simple decision would be so difficult to fulfill. I was sixteen years old, I hadn't had a boyfriend, and I didn't know the Lord Jesus or what his word said about virginity or marriage. It was difficult, because when you fall in love, you're afraid of losing the person you love.

But we must also understand that if a person who really loves you, they will never ask you to do something wrong or harm you. Otherwise, even if it hurts, we must realize that theydon't love us. We faced many tests when we were a couple, just like everyone else, fighting against fleshly desires, but thankfully God helped us overcome them.

Well, the long-awaited day arrived, I never imagined that my wedding would be so special. We didn't plane have a party since there were a lot of expenses because we had to bring my entire family from the ranch. We had to pay everyone'tickets and buy them new clothes. We only buy the essentials for our apartment. My husband told me not to find godmothers for anything, to limit ourselves to what we had, because we didn't have enough money to prepare a meal for the guests. So, we did that, but a sister from Church told me that I couldn't stop them from blessing us if they wanted to help us, because most sisters wanted to be godmothers of something.

She took care of everything, made a list and surprised us with a great wedding. The arrangement at church was very beautiful, it was arranged by a brother who worked at a hotel; he made some beautiful arrangements. There was also a lot of food, a very large cake, a lot of gifts and, in addition to that, the honeymoon was completely paid for. To be honest, we never expected all that.

I thank God because he touched their hearts, so they would bless us so abundantly. Best of all, my dad walked me down the aisle dressed in white. It was a great satisfaction. I said: "Well, Dad, I kept my promise. It wasn't easy, but God gave me the strength to achieve it." My dad looked very happy. I wanted to devote a whole chapter to this topic of chastity and virginity, because I think it's something very important, both for men and women. It seems like nowadays we're taking these issues very lightly and exposing our children's lives to uncontrolled fleshly passions. We have the power and authority to decide what we want to do with our bodies; that's why God gave us free will.

2 Timothy 1:6-7

Therefore, I remind you to stir up the gift of God, which is in you through the laying on of my hands. For God has not given us the spirit of fear; but of power, and of love, and of a sound mind.

Our success or failure in life depend on our priorities. Our spiritual life works the same way; if we put the principles that God established in first place, he will take care of helping you to fulfill them, because he knows your heart's desire. We have the example of the Hebrew youth: Belteshazzar, Shadrach, Meshach, and Abednego. They decided not to defile themselves with the king's food, nor by worshiping his idols. We all know how they set themselves apart with all the decisions these men made to please God and how he honored them, confirming his decisions through their faith.

He strengthened them in such a way that they were stronger and wiser than the others. He saved them from the fiery furnace and he saved Daniel in the lions' den. These inspirational and motivational stories are found in the book of Daniel. Today, our God continues to do the same with all those who truly want to uphold their principles.

He's the same God of the Hebrew youth; He is the same yesterday, today and forever. We make the difference. If we seek and respect his commandments as they did, we will have the same results. Girls, pretty girls and boys too, be very careful; all the bad decisions we make during our adolescence will have consequences later in life. On the other hand, you'll be rewarded for all the good decisions and you'll enjoy life more. I'm going to give you some advice I gave to my girl. One day, when I went to drop my daughter off at high school, there was a line of women with strollers that went around the block. I asked to a lady: "Do they also have groceries for moms here?" She answered: "No, those are only the girls whose parents can't take care of their babies, because they all got pregnant in school."

Well, when I looked at them, they were a bunch little girl with babies in their strollers. They had heavy backpack with books hanging on one side and a diaper bag on the other side. I couldn't believe it. It made me very sadand emotional. At the same time, it gave me great sense of concern for my girl.

I felt like I was dropping her offat the lions 'den every day advised her and tried to make her realizethings, so she would take care of herself. I want to share a bit of the language we used in the field and the terms we used for animals. For example: Roosters step on chickens to lay eggs. A rooster can step on a lot of chickens that the same day and everyone will be happy because we'll have a lot of eggs for breakfast. The cows, goats, pigs, etc., are taken so a male can get pregnant them. That's very normal in the field and when you want to reproduce animals, but our daughters are a parent's most precious treasure.

They're not a chicken for any cockrooster to want to step on. They are not a goat or a cow for a stallion animal to want to do a ride. For people, there is an order established by God: Marriage forms a home for the procreation and care of children.

Genesis 2:24:

Therefore, a man shall leave his father and his mother, and be joined to his wife: and they shall become one flesh.

That is why there is a civil registry where a piece of paper is signed and they commit themselves before witnesses, to comply with the laws of the land, to share their property, take care of themselves and protect each other for the rest of their lives. In addition, there is a Church where they also go with witnesses and commit themselves before God, to respect each other, to take care of each other, in health and illness, in wealth and poverty, for the rest of their lives or tilldeath do them part. Does anyone think that paper is not important?

If he truly loves you, first meet all the laws established to be by your side for the rest of your life. This is the order and process for people, as human beings. Therefore, do not let anyone treat you like an animal, or force you to do what you do not want. A person who loves always seeks the good of the loved one.

If they force you to do something you don't want to do, they simply don't love you and just want to use you. Deuteronomy 22: 13-30 talks about the commandments God gave Moses regarding the laws of chastity. I'm going to ask you to read it carefully at home.

This was punished strongly, and no one was wandering around looking for a taste of love. A lot of people might say "that only happened in the Old Testament," but what did the Lord Jesus say about that? Well, the Lord Jesus said in:

Matthew 5:17, 27-30

V. 17. Do notthink that I am come to destroy the law, or the prophets: I did not come to destroy, but to fulfill.

27 You have heard that it was said to those of old, you shall not commit adultery.

28 But I say to you, that whoever looksat a woman to lust for her has already committed adultery with her in his heart.

29 And if your right eye causes you to sin, pluck it out, and cast it from you; for it is more profitable for you that one of your members perish, than for your whole body be cast into hell.

30 And if your right hand causes you to sin, cut it off, and cast it from you; for it is profitable for you that one of your members perish, than for your whole body to be cast into hell.

He went even further and said that you need to cut off whatever you can't control, so that sin doesn't drag you to hell. That means that you need to program your mind and not tolerate adultery and fornication.

We also need to be very careful with the way we dress, because men treat you differently based on what you wear. Pretty little girls, now that you have an idea of how important your virginity is, if a boy wants to sleep with you and doesn't want to sign a piece of paper, he's looking at you as if you were a goat, a hen or a cow.

He only wants to use you, without any commitment or responsibility. When you see a boy acting like that, get away from him, because he's acting like an animal, with no respect, principles or morality. You have no future with him; as soon as he gets what he wants, and you get pregnant, he'll run away from you and leave you alone as you face your family's shame and are tied to a lifelong commitment. He'll go and find another chicken that will allow him to do anything with her, without paying the price. Young people, there is a time for everything, be patient. For now, focus on your studies, play a sport and plan big things for your future. Follow the apostle Paul's advice in:

Colossians 3:5-7

Therefore, put to death your members which are on the earth: fornication, uncleanness, passion, evil desire, and covetousness, which is idolatry: Because of these things the wrath of God coming upon the sons of disobedience, in which you also once walked when you lived in them.

The apostle Paul says that these things evoke the wrath of God, and if we stir his anger, even if we don't like to hear it, there will be consequences, we will be disciplined.

Hebrews 12:5-11 says:

5. And you have forgotten the exhortation which speaks to you as to son: My son, do not despise the chastening of the Lord, nor be discouraged when you are rebuked of him:

6. For whom the Lord loves He chastens and scourges every son whom He received.

7. If you endure chastening, God deals with you as with sons; for what son is he whom a father does not chasten?

8. But if youare without chasten, of which all have become partakers, then are illegitimate, and not sons.

9. Furthermore, we have had human fathers who corrected us, and we gave them respect. Shall we not much more readily be in subjection to the Father of spirits, and live?

10. For they indeed for a few days chastened us as seemed best to then, but He for our profit, that we may be partakers of his holiness.

11. *Now no chastening seems to be joyful for the present, but grievous; nevertheless, afterward it yields the peaceable fruit of righteousness to thosewho have been trained by it.*

The apostle Paul gives us this advice, so we can avoid the being disciplined by the Lord:

1 Timothy 6:11, 14-15

But you, man of God, flee these things; and follow righteousness, godliness, faith, love, patience, gentleness.

V14 that you keep this commandment without spot, blameless, until our Lord Jesus Christ appearing,

V15 which He will manifest on His own time, He who is the blessed and only Potentate, the King of kings, and Lord of lords.

The apostle Paul was giving this advice to a boy named Timothy. This is also for young people and all men who want to please God. Don't let yourselves be trapped by temptations; run away. There's a saying that says, "it is better run away and live to fight another day." "A little mistake" can cost you your reputation, your testimony and your family's respect. Genesis 39: 7 – 23 says Joseph, the dreamer, ran away to avoid being tempted his master's wife.

He always tried to respect God's principles and he honored him in everything he did. We have all gone through these kinds of temptations in our adolescence, but you must decide if you want to wrap yourself up in them or run away from them. When you want to do things right, God gives you his grace and everyone around you lends you a hand.

God is our heavenly Father and he is more interested in our wellbeing than we can imagine. God's love for you is about a thousand times more than any of your parents' love. When I experienced God's love for the first time, it surpassed my father's love completely. God loves all his children just as much. When you feel this kind of love from God, you love yourself because you understand how valuable you are, and you don't allow yourself to be manipulated or influenced with crumbs of love just, so someone can control and use you. Keep this close to your heart. "Love is respect and it always wants what's best for the person you love."

I made that promise to my earthly father, but now that I know what God says in his word, I wanted to share this with you and motivate you to make that same promise to your heavenly father. He is our eternal father and what greater honor than to promise him that you'll walk down the aisle dressed in white.

In the end, you will benefit from this the most, because your decisions demonstrate your convictions and, therefore, determine your communion with God. He's aware of everything that affects us, that's why he always tries to lead us on the right path. All his commandments are for our own good. One day, as I was praying, the Lord told me: "The problem with many men is that they want to buy a woman, but a woman cannot be bought; a woman must be courted, because her value lies in her dignity. But if a woman sells herself for money, then it she is worthless."

Little pretty girls, single women, widows or those of you who are divorced: Your dignity is invaluable. Wait for someone to pursue you and, no matter what your condition may be, stay strong until the day you walk down the aisle dressed in white. We can all demand that for our dignity.

You will enjoy the reward of your own value and don't let anyone touch you inappropriately way. He will value you even more for that. Be sure about your convictions, because God will always honor those who honor him.

A Letter to God

Dear God:

You are our eternal Father, our God, King and Lord. Thank you for your beloved Son Jesus and for your Holy Spirit. You want us to be like him and recognize him as our older brother, the King of kings and Lord of lords, as our savior because he paid the price for all of us with his blood, so we might all become a part of your family and enjoy it throughout eternity. Father, you use different circumstances in life to shape us so that we are strong and sensitive at the same time, in order to understand others' pain. I pray that the young people will keep your word in their hearts and see your purpose for them, so you may transform the world through them. Father, thank you for your infinite love and your everlasting mercy. Amen.